Intersections

Health and the Built Environment

Urban Land Institute
Building Healthy Places Initiative

About the Urban Land Institute

The Urban Land Institute is a nonprofit research and education organization whose mission is to provide leadership in the responsible use of land and in creating and sustaining thriving communities worldwide.

The Institute maintains a membership representing a broad spectrum of interests and sponsors a wide variety of educational programs and forums to encourage an open exchange of ideas and sharing of experience. ULI initiates research that anticipates emerging land use trends and issues, provides advisory services, and publishes a wide variety of materials to disseminate information on land use development.

Established in 1936, the Institute today has nearly 30,000 members and associates from some 92 countries, representing the entire spectrum of the land use and development disciplines. Professionals represented include developers, builders, property owners, investors, architects, public officials, planners, real estate brokers, appraisers, attorneys, engineers, financiers, academics, students, and librarians.

ULI relies heavily on the experience of its members. It is through member involvement and information resources that ULI has been able to set standards of excellence in development practice. The Institute is recognized internationally as one of America's most respected and widely quoted sources of objective information on urban planning, growth, and development.

Recommended bibliographical listing:
Urban Land Institute. *Intersections: Health and the Built Environment.* Washington, D.C.: Urban Land Institute, 2013.

ISBN: 978-0-87420-282-3

About the Building Healthy Places Initiative

Around the world, communities face pressing health challenges related to the built environment. For many years, ULI and its members have been active players in discussions and projects that make the link between human health and development; we know that health is a core component of thriving communities.

In January 2013, ULI's Board of Directors approved a focus on healthy communities as a two-year cross-disciplinary theme for the organization.

Through the Building Healthy Places Initiative, ULI is leveraging the power of its global networks to shape **projects and places** in ways that improve the health of **people and communities**. The organization is focusing on four main areas of impact:

- **Awareness.** Raise awareness of the connections between health and the built environment in the real estate community, working to ensure that health is a mainstream consideration.
- **Tools.** Develop or share tools—including best practices, criteria, and other materials—that define and advance approaches to healthy buildings, projects, and communities.
- **Value.** Build understanding of the market and nonmarket factors at play in building healthy places, and the value proposition of building and operating in health-promoting ways.
- **Commitments.** Gain commitments from members and others, including local governments, to work, build, and operate in more health-promoting ways.

Learn more and connect: http://www.uli.org/health.

Share your story via Twitter: #ulihealth.

About This Report

Intersections: Health and the Built Environment explores the relationship between how healthy we are and the way our buildings and communities function. We can build our way to better health, it proposes, by changing our approach to cities, communities, and places. As real estate leaders and stewards of the built environment, we can do more to improve lives and foster healthy outcomes. And along the way, we can create places of enduring value.

ULI Senior Executives

Patrick Phillips
Chief Executive Officer

Cheryl Cummins
Executive Officer

Michael Terseck
Chief Financial Officer/Chief Administrative Officer

Joe Montgomery
Chief Executive, Europe

David Howard
Executive Vice President, Development and ULI Foundation

Kathleen Carey
Executive Vice President/Chief Content Officer

Lela Agnew
Executive Vice President, Communications

Marilee Utter
Executive Vice President, District Councils

Principal Author

Kathleen McCormick
Fountainhead Communications LLC
Boulder, Colorado

Contributing Authors

Rachel MacCleery
Senior Vice President, Content

Sara Hammerschmidt
Associate, Content

ULI Project Staff

Rachel MacCleery
Senior Vice President, Content

Sara Hammerschmidt
Associate, Content

Basil Hallberg
Senior Research Associate

Ed McMahon
Senior Resident Fellow, Environment

Maureen McAvey
Senior Resident Fellow, Retail

Sarah Jo Peterson
Senior Policy Director

James Mulligan
Managing Editor

Joanne Platt
Publications Professionals LLC
Manuscript Editor

Betsy VanBuskirk
Creative Director

Deanna Pineda
Muse Advertising Design
Graphic Designer

Craig Chapman
Senior Director
Publishing Operations

Cover Letter

Dear Reader,

The built environment is part of the health problem. But it is also part of the solution.

That is the main message of *Intersections: Health and the Built Environment*, an important new report from ULI. As the world grapples with a host of health problems—including the growing toll of chronic disease, air and water pollution, and surging health care costs—we, the developers, builders, designers, and financiers of the built environment, are being looked to for solutions.

We know a lot about how to craft cities, communities, and projects that help foster healthier outcomes for people. Opportunities for active transportation, accessible and attractive staircases, proximity to nature and transit—all have been shown to improve health. And by responding to market demands, healthy places also help generate economic value. We know that health is a core component of thriving communities.

But there is still a lot we can learn. And when it comes to public health, there are many untapped opportunities to do more. That is why ULI has launched the Building Healthy Places Initiative, which will leverage the power of ULI's global networks to shape projects and places in ways that improve the health of people and communities.

Over the course of the initiative, public health topics will be threaded through ULI's convenings, publications, research, partnerships, and conversations. We will be sharing stories about innovative projects and approaches, learning from each other and from experts in the field, and seeking to advance understanding of what works when it comes to health.

We *can* build our way to better health. ULI members are in the business of improving the places in which we live our lives. Through a better understanding of the complex health challenges we face, and through putting our knowledge into practice in the decisions we make as stewards of the built environment, we can promote health—one project, and one community, at a time.

Lynn Thurber
Urban Land Institute Chairman

Patrick Phillips
Urban Land Institute Chief Executive Officer

Contents

Chapter 1: We Can Build Our Way to Better Health 2

ULI Leadership for Healthy Places 5
U.S. Health Trends: Troubling Directions 6
Health and Income 8
The Healthy Place Opportunity 11

Chapter 2: Moving in the Wrong Direction? Global Health Trends 12

The Rise of Chronic Disease 14
Trends Influencing Health 16
A Path Forward 23

Chapter 3: Better Health through Community Design 24

Smart Growth: Building toward Health and Saving Money 26
The Power of Parks and Trails 29
Aging in Place: It Never Gets Old 31
School's (Too Far) Out 32

Chapter 4: Active Transportation 34

Transportation That Gets Us Moving 36
Complete Streets: A Safe Bet 43
Shared Cars and Car-Free Zones 43
Slimming Down Parking 44

Chapter 5: Healthy Buildings, Healthy People 46

Location Choices 48
Greener, Healthier Buildings 48
Designing for Active Living 52
Reworking Workplaces 53
Healthy Learning Environments 53
Health Care Facilities 55

Chapter 6: Access to Healthy Food 56
Crossing the Food Desert: Grocery Stores 59
Urban Agriculture 63
Chapter 7: Clear Air, Clean Water 64
Air Quality 65
Water for Life 68
Green Infrastructure 71
Adding It All Up: Elements of Healthy Development 74

Information Boxes

Projects That Work for Health

Via Verde, South Bronx, New York ... 9
Heartlands, Cornwall, England ... 17
Mueller, Austin, Texas ... 25
Mariposa, Denver, Colorado ... 28
The Uptown, Oakland, California ... 38
HGST Campus, San Jose, California ... 44
The Bullitt Center, Seattle, Washington ... 49
Googleplex, Mountain View, California ... 54
Alder Hey Children's Health Park, Liverpool, England ... 55
Union Market, Washington, D.C. ... 60
Willowsford, Loudoun County, Virginia ... 61
Silver City Townhomes, Milwaukee, Wisconsin ... 73
Public Utilities Commission Headquarters, San Francisco, California ... 73

Innovations in Health

U.S. Cities Invest in Infrastructure for Health ... 4
Colorado Health Foundation and Colorado Communities ... 7
Upwardly Mobile Medellín, Colombia ... 13
Augustenborg EcoDistrict, Malmö, Sweden ... 23
ULI's Ten Principles for Building Healthy Places ... 27
Being Intentional about Health Outcomes ... 29
Blue Zones Project, Albert Lea, Minnesota ... 29
International Development Banks: $175 Billion for Active Transportation ... 35
Active Design Guidelines for Communities ... 37
Protected Two-Way Bike Lanes in Chicago, Illinois 39
Biking in Copenhagen, Portland, and Hangzhou ... 40
Global Programs for Sustainable and Healthy Buildings and Communities ... 48
Active Design Guidelines for Buildings ... 52
Urban Farming, Detroit, Michigan ... 57
Fresh Food Retailer Initiative, New Orleans, Louisiana ... 59
Healthy Food Chain, Boulder, Colorado ... 60
Urban Gardens, Cape Town, South Africa ... 63
Clearing the Air in Mexico City, Mexico ... 68
Community Sanitation Blocks, Mumbai, India ... 69
Watershed Management Group and Tucson's Green Streets Policy ... 71

Insights from the Experts

Jonathan Rose, President, Jonathan Rose Companies LLC ... 10
Dr. Richard Jackson, Chair, Department of Environmental Health Sciences, University of California, Los Angeles ... 33
Bert Gregory, Chairman and CEO, Mithun ... 51
Simon Ng, Head of Transport and Sustainability Research, Civic Exchange, Hong Kong ... 67

Acronyms

APTA	American Public Transportation Association
BREEAM	Building Research Establishment Environmental Assessment Method
BRT	bus rapid transit
CSA	community-supported agriculture
CSO	combined sewer overflow
EPA	Environmental Protection Agency
GDP	gross domestic product
HDMT	Healthy Development Measurement Tool
HIA	Health Impact Assessment
LEED	Leadership in Energy and Environmental Design
LEED-ND	Leadership in Energy and Environmental Design for Neighborhood Development
MDB	multilateral development bank
STAR	Sustainability Tools for Assessing and Rating
VMT	vehicle miles traveled
VOC	volatile organic compound

CHAPTER 1

We Can Build Our Way to Better Health

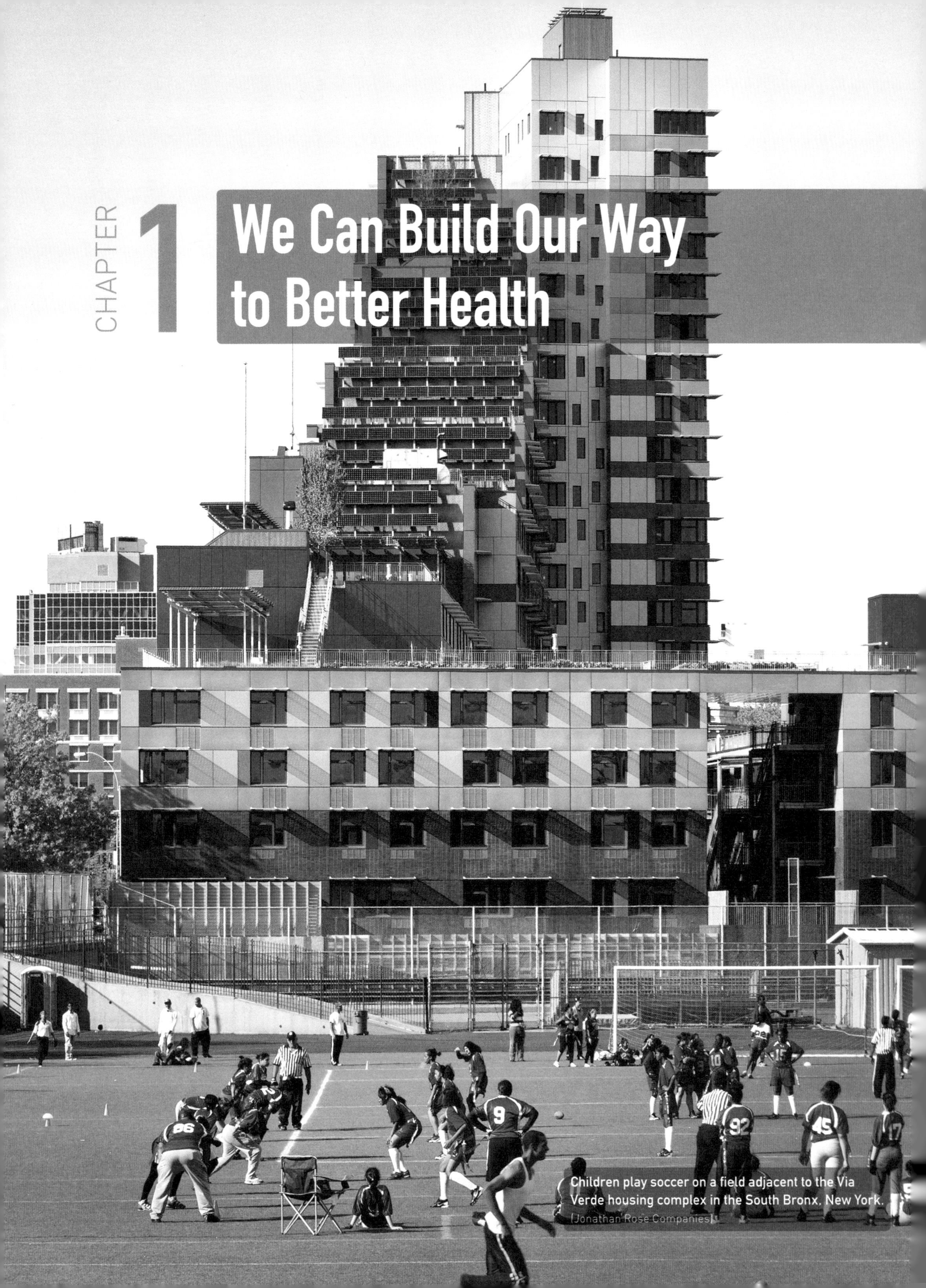

Children play soccer on a field adjacent to the Via Verde housing complex in the South Bronx, New York. (Jonathan Rose Companies)

In the 21st century, as the world meets the demands of population growth, increasing urban development, and climate change, we face new challenges in public health. Public health is no longer solely the business of health professionals: public officials, urban planners, transportation decision makers, architects, landscape architects, builders, and real estate developers all have a role to play in addressing public health challenges.

Many of today's health challenges are driven by chronic or "lifestyle" diseases, including cardiovascular and respiratory diseases, type 2 diabetes, and cancer. These diseases now cause nearly two-thirds of deaths worldwide each year. By 2030, chronic diseases will cause 52 million global deaths per year, nearly five times the number of deaths from communicable diseases.

Epidemic rates of chronic disease have become a drag on the economies and futures of families, communities, nations, and whole regions. The growing cost of health care is a global megatrend that is making us rethink land use and transportation patterns. Health is becoming a competitive advantage or disadvantage for cities.

With this shift, market opportunities are emerging to change the way we design and build so that we support healthy living and vibrant economies. Like demographics, opportunities to be healthy are influencing what people want in their homes, workplaces, schools, public spaces, and communities. People care about their health. So what does that add up to for real estate?

Health is a state of complete physical, mental, and social well-being and not merely the absence of disease or infirmity.

—World Health Organization

What Is a Healthy Place?

ULI believes that healthy places are designed, built, and programmed to support the physical, mental, and social well-being of the people who live, work, learn, and visit there.

Healthy places

- offer healthy and affordable housing options, and a variety of safe, comfortable, and convenient transportation choices;
- provide access to healthy foods, the natural environment, and other amenities that allow people to reach their full potential;
- are designed thoughtfully, with an eye to making the healthy choice the easy choice, and they are built using health-promoting materials; and
- address unique community issues with innovative and sustainable solutions.

Benches on the Calligraphy Greenway in Taichung, Taiwan, provide respite for visitors. (AECOM)

INNOVATIONS IN HEALTH

U.S. Cities Invest in Infrastructure for Health

Campaigns by U.S. cities to encourage exercise to combat obesity include the following:

Oklahoma City, Oklahoma. Worried that major companies were bypassing his city because of its health issues, Oklahoma City's mayor Mick Cornett challenged city residents in 2008 to lose 1 million pounds. Cornett contributed to the goal by losing 43 pounds himself. The "This City Is Going on a Diet" campaign was backed with investments in trails and programs that linked parks and recreation facilities.

The city has also made a series of health-promoting investments in its downtown. The latest set of improvements are funded by a one-cent sales tax increase, which is channeling $777 million into a 70-acre central park, 57 miles of new multiuse trails, and recreation upgrades for the Oklahoma River.

Atlanta, Georgia. Atlanta's BeltLine is a revitalization and active-community project with an ambitious set of physical activity–promoting amenities like public parks, multiuse trails, and transportation options. The BeltLine reuses 22 miles of historic railroad corridors circling downtown Atlanta and connects 45 neighborhoods to each other and to the entire Atlanta region through enhanced transit offerings.

When completed, the project will have developed 33 miles of multiuse trails, 1,300 acres of parks, and 5,600 units of affordable housing.

Tax allocation district funding that anchors the 25-year financial plan has provided $120 million since 2005. An additional $179.5 million has been invested from private and local government sources.

Market demands from millennials and baby boomers are helping usher in active-living urban development. Millennials in particular express strong preferences for more compact, walkable, mixed-use, and mixed-income communities. They want amenities like storage for exercise equipment within buildings and easy access to parks and open space.

Overwhelmingly, baby boomers and older people want to age in place. They want housing and communities that can meet their needs as they grow older. And across the generations, demand is strong for communities with transit and other elements that support active living.

Atlanta Mayor Kasim Reed inaugurates the BeltLine's Eastside Trail in October 2012 with a community bike ride. (Christopher T. Martin)

Living and Working Conditions in Homes and Communities Influence Health

Factors influencing health

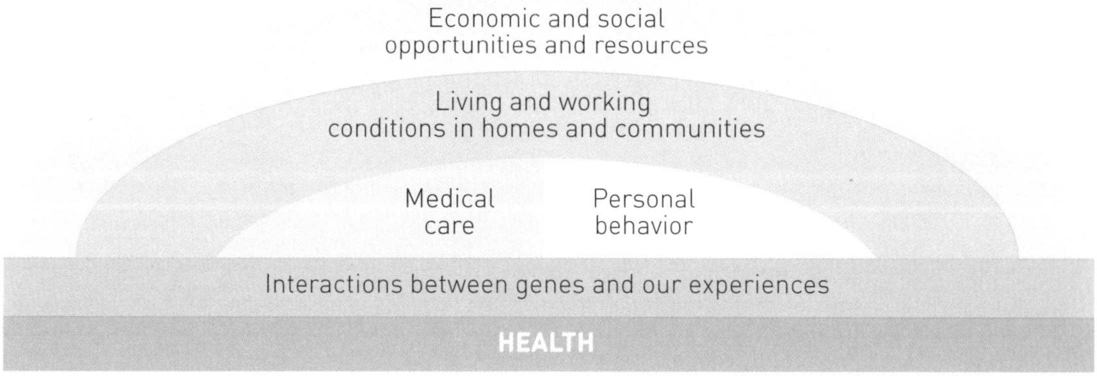

Source: Robert Wood Johnson Foundation.

Health presents a market opportunity for forward-thinking developers and real estate leaders, and the market presents an opportunity to help shape communities in health-promoting ways.

Research points to how buildings, roads, and neighborhood design affect human health. When devising strategies for the built environment to improve health, we can also draw from decades of work on smart growth—many smart-growth approaches for the design, construction, management, and programming of communities also work for health.

ULI Leadership for Healthy Places

For many years, ULI and its members have been active players in discussions and projects that make the link between human health and development; we know that health is a core component of thriving communities. Through the Building Healthy Places Initiative, ULI is leveraging the power of its global networks to shape projects and places in ways that improve the health of people and communities.

Professionals involved in land use have a powerful role to play in creating healthy places. ULI members can lead in building healthier environments in the following ways:

- **Through their organizations,** by following principles of planning, design, and construction that incorporate healthy and sustainable practices, and by setting an example with healthy work environments and policies that encourage fitness and healthy eating;
- **As a fundamental consideration in development projects,** by incorporating elements that enhance health and the environment, such as selecting development sites with public transit access; building in compact ways, including amenities that promote healthy lifestyles; and using healthy building materials; and
- **Through their influence on policy,** by working with local and national governments, regional transportation agencies, foundations and community groups, and business, health care, education, and civic leaders to create land use, zoning, and building frameworks that are conducive to healthy lives.

The good news is that the real estate industry is getting on board. A summer 2013

ULI Members Agree That Health and the Built Environment Are Linked

Responses to ULI member survey conducted in July 2013

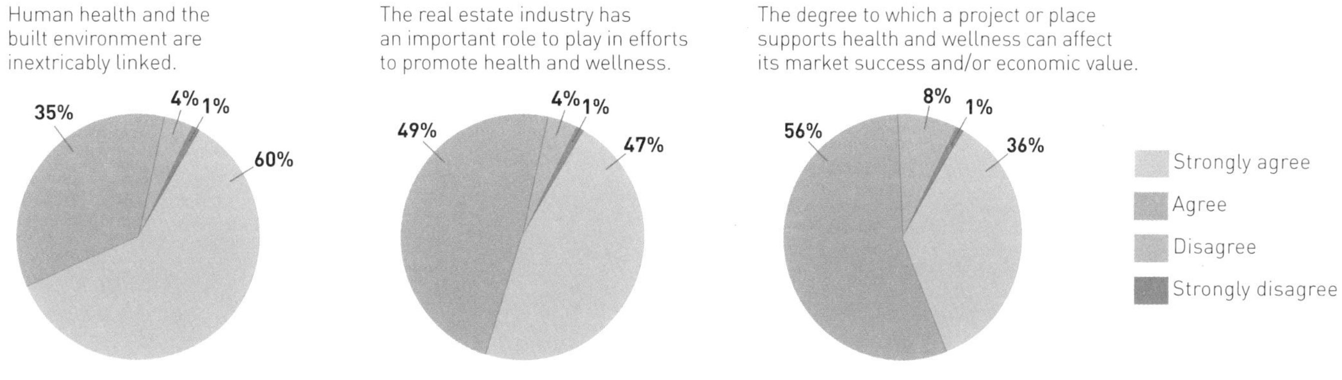

Source: Urban Land Institute.

U.S. Obesity Rates Increased Dramatically between 1990 and 2010

Obesity trends among U.S. adults

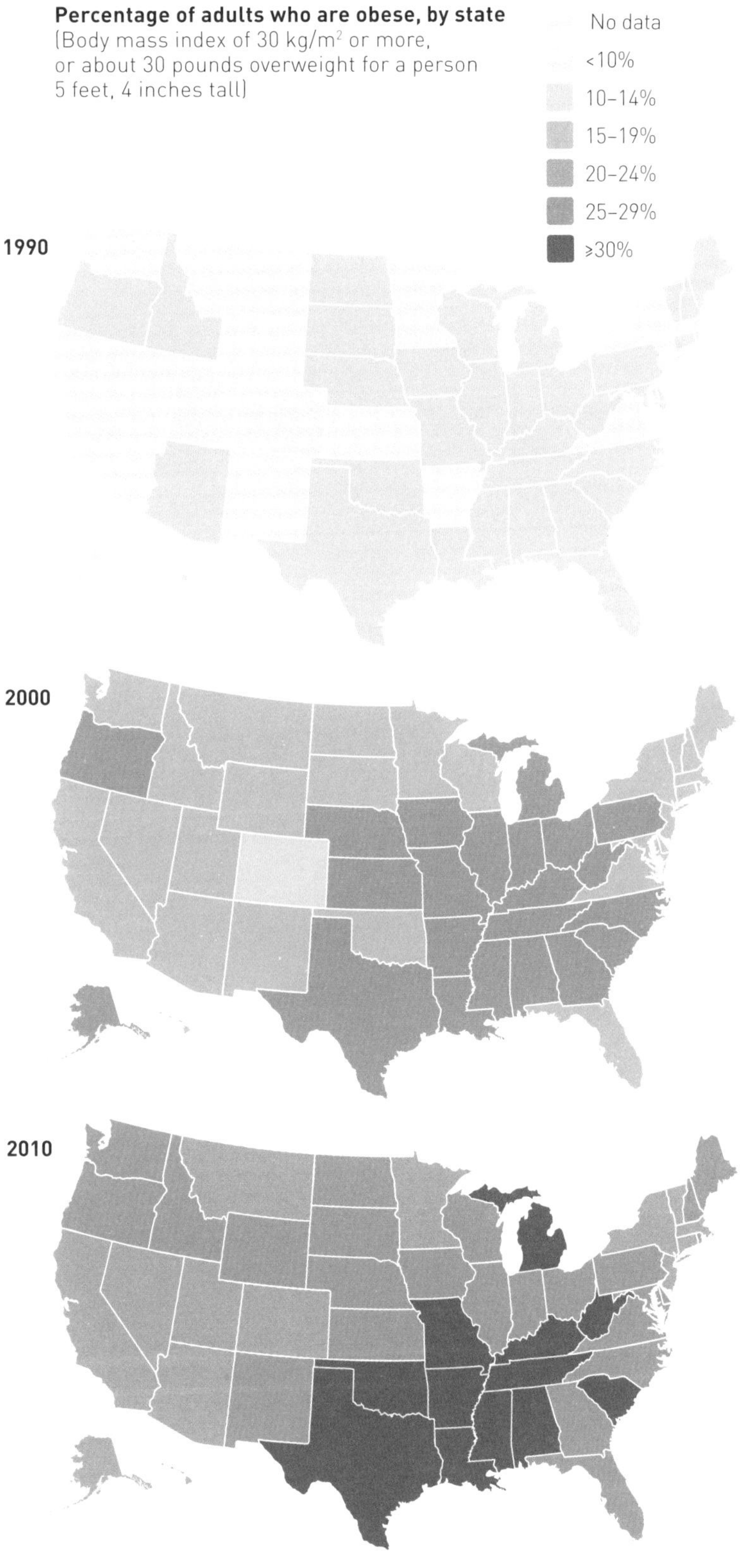

Source: U.S. Centers for Disease Control and Prevention.

survey of ULI members found that the majority understand linkages between health and the built environment; 96 percent strongly agreed that the real estate industry has an important role to play.

U.S. Health Trends: Troubling Directions

The bad news is that major health trends in the U.S. are heading in the wrong direction, despite recent encouraging signs, including modest improvements in children's weight and activity levels. In the United States, a huge and growing portion of wealth and economic activ-

BY THE NUMBERS

The High Costs of Poor Health in the United States

$147 billion
Annual cost of the U.S. obesity epidemic

75% Percentage of U.S. health expenditures attributed to treating chronic disease

19.2% Projected percentage of U.S. GDP that will be spent on health care by 2020, up from 7.2% in 1970

$5.6 billion
Annual U.S. health care costs related to obesity that could be saved if one in ten adults started a walking program

Sources: U.S. Centers for Disease Control and Prevention; U.S. Centers for Medicare & Medicaid Services; Alliance for Biking and Walking.

ity is directed toward treating disease. These expenses have the potential to squeeze out spending on more productive endeavors.

Here are some disturbing U.S. statistics:

- Health care expenditures—a projected $3 trillion in 2014—will consume 19 percent of the nation's gross domestic product by 2020, according to federal projections.
- Three-quarters of U.S. health care spending goes toward treating chronic diseases.
- Health care will require an investment of over $9,000 per person in 2014, more than any other country. The lives of U.S. residents, however, are nearly five years shorter than what would be expected with such a high level of expenditure.
- The U.S. adult obesity rate, now affecting one in three adults, could reach 43 percent by 2018, generating $344 billion annually in health care costs related to type 2 diabetes, hypertension, and related diseases.

Can we turn the tide on these troubling health trends? It will be a daunting task. But the success of the U.S. campaign against tobacco over the past four decades—smoking has declined in use from 37 percent of adults to 19 percent—inspires those working to bend the arc of U.S. health trends.

INNOVATIONS IN HEALTH

Colorado Health Foundation and Colorado Communities

Colorado is a magnet for millennials and others drawn by the natural environment and active lifestyle, which in turn produce economic benefits for the state: bicycling, for example, pumps over $1 billion into state coffers.

In 2009, however, Colorado spent $1.6 billion treating conditions related to obesity. Reflecting rising obesity rates across the nation, some 21 percent of Colorado's adults and 14 percent of its children are obese.

The Colorado Health Foundation, supported by a $2.2 billion endowment, is trying to reverse this trend to make Colorado "the healthiest state in the nation." The foundation supports projects such as Mariposa, a healthy affordable-housing community in Denver.

To reinforce the connection between a healthy built environment and economic development, the foundation partnered with ULI to conduct Advisory Services panels in three Colorado communities, the first step in an extended engagement process between the foundation and the communities aimed at increasing physical activity and fostering healthy outcomes among residents.

The Advisory Services panels in Colorado recommended strategies to foster active living in three communities.

Health Care Expenditures Are Claiming a Larger and Larger Share of U.S. GDP

U.S. national health expenditures as a percentage of gross domestic product, by decade

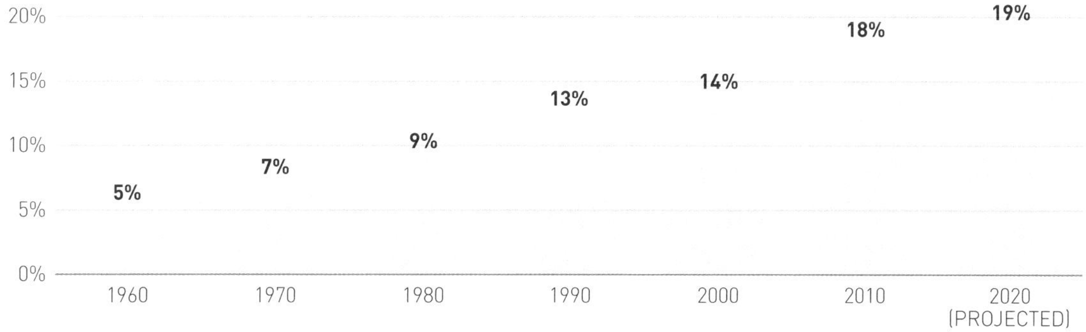

Source: U.S. Centers for Medicare & Medicaid Services, Office of the Actuary.
Note: The projection for 2020 includes impacts of the Affordable Care Act.

BY THE NUMBERS

Chronic Health Concerns and Children

1 in 3 Share of U.S. children considered overweight or obese

500% Increase in fast food consumption among U.S. children since 1970

5 Number of years by which obesity threatens to shorten the lives of U.S. children

13 million Number of missed U.S. school days each year due to asthma-related illnesses

Sources: American Institute of Architects; Boston Children's Hospital; U.S. Department of Health and Human Services; U.S. Environmental Protection Agency.

To work, efforts must be comprehensive and must focus not just on health care delivery but on all the forces shaping health, including the built environment.

Health and Income

Household income levels, educational attainment, and race are important factors in the health picture. Although the built environment is not the whole story here, it is part of the story. Higher incomes can translate into better access to nutritious food, safe neighborhoods, recreational opportunities, and other elements of healthy lifestyles.

Life expectancy, infant mortality, child and adult health, and other indicators are all affected by income, education, and racial background. Efforts to ensure that all people live in health-promoting communities, with access to healthy food, safe streets, high-quality parks, and stable and healthy housing, as well as pursuit of other strategies discussed in this report, can help address and alleviate these disparities.

Health Outcomes Vary across Income Levels and by Racial and Ethnic Group

Percentage of U.S. adults in poor or fair health (age-adjusted)

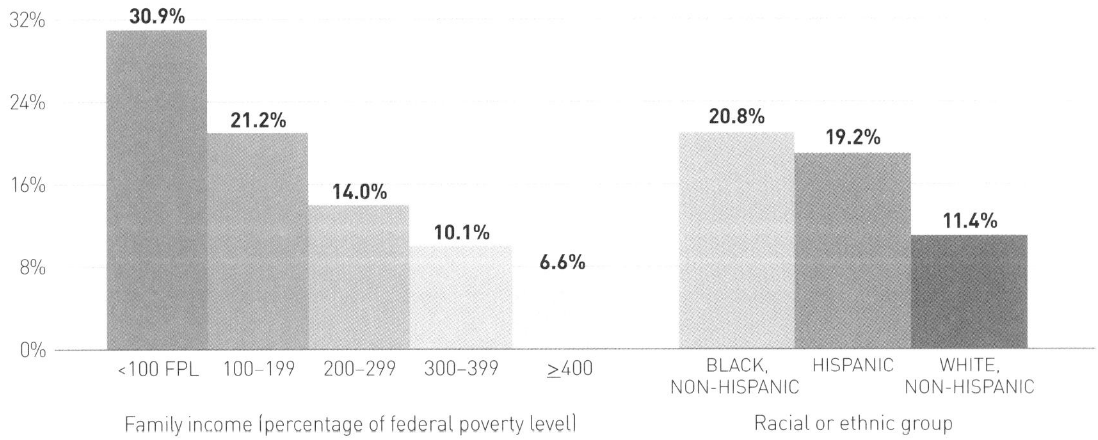

Source: Robert Wood Johnson Foundation.

The courtyard at the Station Center housing complex in Union City, California, includes community gardens and a play area. (Bruce Damonte)

BY THE NUMBERS

The Built Environment and Physical Activity

67% Percentage of the U.S. workforce that is overweight or obese

47% Increased likelihood that people who live in neighborhoods with sidewalks get at least 30 minutes of exercise per day

50% Increased likelihood that people who live near trails meet physical activity guidelines

Sources: Public Health Institute; Active Living Research.

PROJECTS THAT WORK FOR HEALTH

Via Verde, South Bronx, New York

Jonathan Rose Companies LLC, a New York–based multidisciplinary planning and development firm, is noted for holistic projects that embody aspects of healthy living. A recent project, Via Verde/The Green Way, won the New Housing New York Legacy Competition and ULI's Jack Kemp Workforce Housing Models of Excellence Award.

The $98 million Via Verde, codeveloped with Phipps Houses and designed by the partnership of Dattner Architects and Grimshaw, features 294,000 square feet of mixed-use construction on 1.5 acres close to transit. Completed in 2012, the project has 222 mixed-income rental and co-op residential units, 7,500 square feet of retail and community facility space, and 40,000 square feet of green roofs and open space.

At its heart is a garden that serves as the organizing element and spiritual identity for the community. The green roofs and open space, located on connected low-rise townhomes, a mid-rise duplex building, and a 20-story tower, are used to harvest rainwater and grow fruits and vegetables. The LEED Gold project features other healthy living amenities, such as open-air courtyards, a health education and wellness center, a community medical clinic, a fitness center, and bicycle storage.

Rooftop vegetable gardens can be found at the Via Verde housing complex in the South Bronx, New York. (Jonathan Rose Companies)

INSIGHTS FROM THE EXPERTS

Jonathan Rose, President, Jonathan Rose Companies LLC

Jonathan F.P. Rose, president of Jonathan Rose Companies LLC, has built a reputation for thinking outside the box to develop holistic projects that embody principles of diversity, environmental responsibility, livelihood, and interdependence.

Q: *What are the key elements of a healthy community?*

A: A healthy community begins with housing, which is the platform for physical, cognitive, and social health. But we also need to recognize that a community is more than a building—it includes its context. Communities of opportunity include both the physical and social infrastructure for well-being, including multiple transportation options; safe, affordable, healthy, and green housing; affordable healthy food; access to health care, jobs, education and training, and social and physical connections; and culture. Enterprise Community Partners has advanced these principles for low-income communities, but they really apply to all communities—urban, suburban, rural—and at all economic levels.

> *In our experience, green, walkable, mixed-income, mixed-use communities like Highlands' Garden Village in Denver are increasingly what the market is looking for.*
>
> *—Jonathan Rose*

Q: *What specifically can ULI members do to improve the health of the built environment?*

A: They can start by building healthier, greener, more diverse communities in the right locations: connected places served by existing infrastructure and community resources. Human health is dependent on a healthy natural environment, and so it's essential that we reduce the environmental impact of development. If we don't, the outcome is the extraordinary pollution evident in cities such as Guangzhou and Beijing. The internal environment of our buildings must also be healthy, with clean fresh air, daylight, healthy building materials, and reduced energy consumption. Taken together, making buildings and citywide environments healthier will improve well-being.

Q: *What should ULI members consider about return on investment for healthy communities?*

A: In our experience, green, walkable, mixed-income, mixed-use communities like Highlands' Garden Village in Denver are increasingly what the market is looking for. Projects that fail to address these market drivers are more likely to underperform. We're seeing emerging new standards of best practice for green and healthy projects. In our experience, healthier communities have lower turnover and higher occupancy. Many of these strategies do not cost more, but just take more time to think through, using integrated design and planning. They may cost more on the infrastructure side, but that is balanced by cost savings in social services and health care.

The Healthy Place Opportunity

Thinking about the relationship between health and the built environment is not new. In the 19th and 20th centuries, architects and planners in London, New York, and Paris joined with public health professionals and social reformers to reduce infectious diseases by designing buildings, streets, parks, neighborhoods, and clean water systems to improve health.

Now, the built environment is once again an important part of the solution to today's public health crisis. ULI members are helping create active, green, and sustainable environments that are healthy for people and that add value to real estate.

As the ULI member survey shows, many ULI members understand that the design and programming of a neighborhood or building affect both its **health** and its **value**. Demographic trends, including the preferences of millennials, baby boomers, and other groups, are driving real estate practice.

Projects and communities that can respond to growing market demands for transportation that supports active lifestyles, for housing types that allow people to age in place, and for a mix of uses and other elements that promote health will see their value endure over time.

Meeting the demand for healthy living will require new development features, as well as investment in strategies that have proven returns, like parks. What are the emerging opportunities to meet the needs and desires of the marketplace and improve health at the same time? Savvy developers, planners, and communities will be paying attention.

The new Amazon headquarters in Seattle includes rain gardens, a green roof, and an exterior green wall.
(Benjamin Benschneider)

CHAPTER 2

Moving in the Wrong Direction? Global Health Trends

Raised wooden boardwalks through wetland ponds in Nanhu Eco-City Central Park in Tangshan, China, increase interactions with plants and wildlife. (Beijing Tsinghua Tongheng Urban Planning & Design Institute)

Human health is affected by many factors, such as the foods we eat, the air we breathe, the water we drink, and whether we can walk or bike to work or school. Health is also influenced by such factors as human choice and behavior, as well as genetics, access to health care, transportation, housing, education, income, and whether the environment is safe and promotes health.

Half the world's population now lives in cities. And although urbanization is generally associated with increasing prosperity and good health, rapid migration from rural areas and enormous population growth are putting more pressure on infrastructure for food, water, housing, health care, open space, and other elements that contribute to healthy environments.

INNOVATIONS IN HEALTH

Upwardly Mobile Medellín, Colombia

In 2012, Medellín was recognized for having one of the best transportation systems in the world by the Institute for Transportation and Development Policy, a global consortium for sustainable transportation. The city has come a long way in the 20 years since it was branded the murder capital of the world.

A major driver of Medellín's transformation has been an innovative transportation system that provides access to jobs, educational opportunities, and civic and recreational spaces for residents living in the city's poor hillside *favelas*, or slums.

The centerpiece is Metro de Medellín, a network of clean efficient train cars that serves over 500,000 passengers daily. Financed by a public/private partnership, the transit network includes cable cars and a 1,263-foot outdoor escalator that carry *favela* residents up and down the steep hillsides, saving hours of travel time to reach jobs, health care, schools, and services.

The metro's transit hubs have spurred new investment in infrastructure, services, and amenities, such as hospitals and police stations, many integrated into the metro infrastructure. The transit system benefits from new connections with new public green spaces and pedestrian routes, a public bike-share program linked to universities, and a rideshare/carpool program involving more than 170 institutions.

Medellín, Colombia's cable car system, opened in 2010, has revolutionized access and mobility for the city's poorest residents. (Jess Zimbabwe)

BY THE NUMBERS

The High Costs of Poor Health

4.3% Percentage of China's GDP spent on health costs attributed to air and water pollution

9% Average percentage of GDP spent on health by European Union countries

$240 billion Estimated national income India will forgo between 2005 and 2010 because of premature deaths caused by heart disease, stroke, and diabetes

52 million Number of lives that by 2030 will be claimed each year by chronic disease globally

Sources: World Bank; Organization for Economic Cooperation and Development and European Commission; World Health Organization.

Health impacts from the design of the built environment are a global concern. Many health challenges are directly related to transportation choices, land use patterns, infrastructure, and accessibility. And many opportunities exist to shift our approaches to designing and developing buildings, neighborhoods, and infrastructure to reverse chronic disease trends and improve public health.

The Rise of Chronic Disease

Certain chronic diseases that used to affect only wealthier populations in the developed world are "spreading" to countries undergoing rapid urban development and the lifestyle

Grass and wooden decking at the Marco Polo Terraces, a new public open space at the HafenCity development in Hamburg, Germany, invites visitors to stop and rest. [Thomas Hampel/Elbe & Flut]

changes that go with it. Chronic diseases now outpace infectious diseases in every global region except Africa, where rates are also rising. These diseases are responsible for two-thirds of deaths worldwide. By 2030, chronic disease rates will increase by nearly 50 percent, claiming the lives of 52 million people. Ischemic heart disease, caused in part by high cholesterol and diabetes, is the number one cause of death worldwide.

Global populations are also aging as a result of public health efforts to curb infectious diseases. Urban populations face growing environmental threats and changing lifestyle patterns, such as physical inactivity and unhealthy habits related to food, alcohol, and tobacco.

BY THE NUMBERS

The High Impact of Chronic Disease

2 in 3 Share of deaths worldwide caused by chronic diseases

300% Increase in the prevalence of obesity in Europe since the 1980s

366 million Projected number of people with diabetes worldwide by 2030; 80% are projected to be living in developing countries

1 in 3 Share of U.S. adults who are obese—the highest rate of obesity in the world

Sources: World Health Organization; Global Health Policy Center at the Center for Strategic and International Studies; U.S. Centers for Disease Control and Prevention.

The Wilmington Waterfront Park near the Port of Los Angeles, California, provides a venue for soccer games. How to reconcile the impacts of ports with health is a global challenge. (Sasaki Associates)

The World Is Becoming Increasingly Urban

Urbanization rates

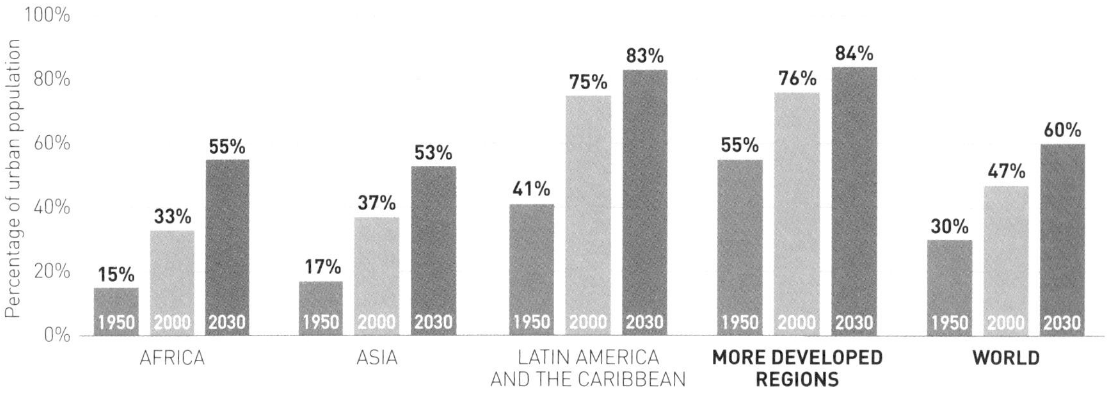

Source: United Nations.

Today, for example, obesity affects one in ten adults globally and one in three adults in the United States. High obesity rates are linked to chronic and often lethal conditions, including coronary heart disease, type 2 diabetes, and certain cancers. Obesity is caused by lifestyle factors, such as the consumption of unhealthy or excessive amounts of food and a lack of activity.

Global obesity rates have doubled since 1980. In the United States, obesity rates have also increased dramatically: in 1990, no state had an obesity rate greater than 15 percent, but by 2010, 12 states had obesity rates greater than 30 percent, and none had rates of less than 20 percent.

Trends Influencing Health

Many trends and factors are influencing health globally.

Population Growth/Urbanization. Global population is expected to increase from 7 billion today to over 9 billion in 2050. In emerging countries such as China and India, rapidly growing populations are increasing pressures on the natural resources that supply energy, food, and water. By 2050, over 70 percent of the world's population will live in cities, according to the World Health Organization.

Aging. Over one-quarter of the population in the 34 member nations of the Organization for Economic Cooperation and Development will be over 65 years old in 2050, compared with 15 percent today. Japan has increased average life expectancy to 84 years, and nearly one-quarter of its population is already over 65. Countries including Germany, Italy, and Greece are not far behind. In the United States, the 65-plus population is expected to double to nearly 72 million by 2030.

Environment. Global greenhouse gas emissions are projected to increase by 50 percent between 2005 and 2025, mostly from energy-related carbon dioxide emissions. Urban air pollution will likely become the top environmental cause of death worldwide by 2050; by then, natural-land biodiversity is expected to decrease by 10 percent.

Climate Change. Climate change–triggered sea level rise and extreme weather events are leading to new patterns of migration and growth and could have a significant impact on economic development, food production, air quality, water supply and quality, sanitation systems, and housing. Buildings will need greater resiliency in the face of rising temperatures, wind and water forces, and power failures.

Lifestyle. Diet and exercise are two major determinants of health. Improving diets through access to affordable healthy food and feeding a growing population will require expansion of agricultural production, which will increase competition for land. Inactivity, a major factor in obesity, stems from excessive time spent in cars and in front of computers, televisions, and digital media. In Europe, for example, where estimates show that physical inactivity causes 1 million deaths annually, only a third of the adult and youth populations are active 30 minutes per day.

PROJECTS THAT WORK FOR HEALTH

Heartlands, Cornwall, England

Heartlands is a £35 million ($55 million) redeveloped mixed-use residential arts community located in the village of Pool in Cornwall. Focused on healthy living through redevelopment, investment, and sustainable design, the 18.5-acre site includes new artist studios, apartments, a community hall, conference facilities, a café/restaurant/bar, and retail shops.

In 2007, the local council won a lottery to develop a low-carbon urban community around a defunct historic mine. An integrated design team led by U.K.-based Buro Happold Ltd engineers with Stride Treglown architects restored the granite mine buildings and turned them into a visitor attraction about the history of Cornish tin mining. Completed in 2011, the award-winning project has become a catalyst for economic development, producing over 75 local jobs and attracting more than 240,000 visitors within the first year.

The community now enjoys active public spaces—a village green, market squares, children's play areas, and events arenas—as well as footpaths and bike trails that lead through gardens and green spaces to the countryside.

Heartlands has transformed a neglected section of Cornwall, England, into a tourist destination, with flex space for artists and mixed-income residences. (David Clapp)

Noncommunicable, Chronic Diseases Are Leading Causes of Death Globally

Data on the Top Ten Global Causes of Death and Other Health Statistics for Selected Countries and Regions

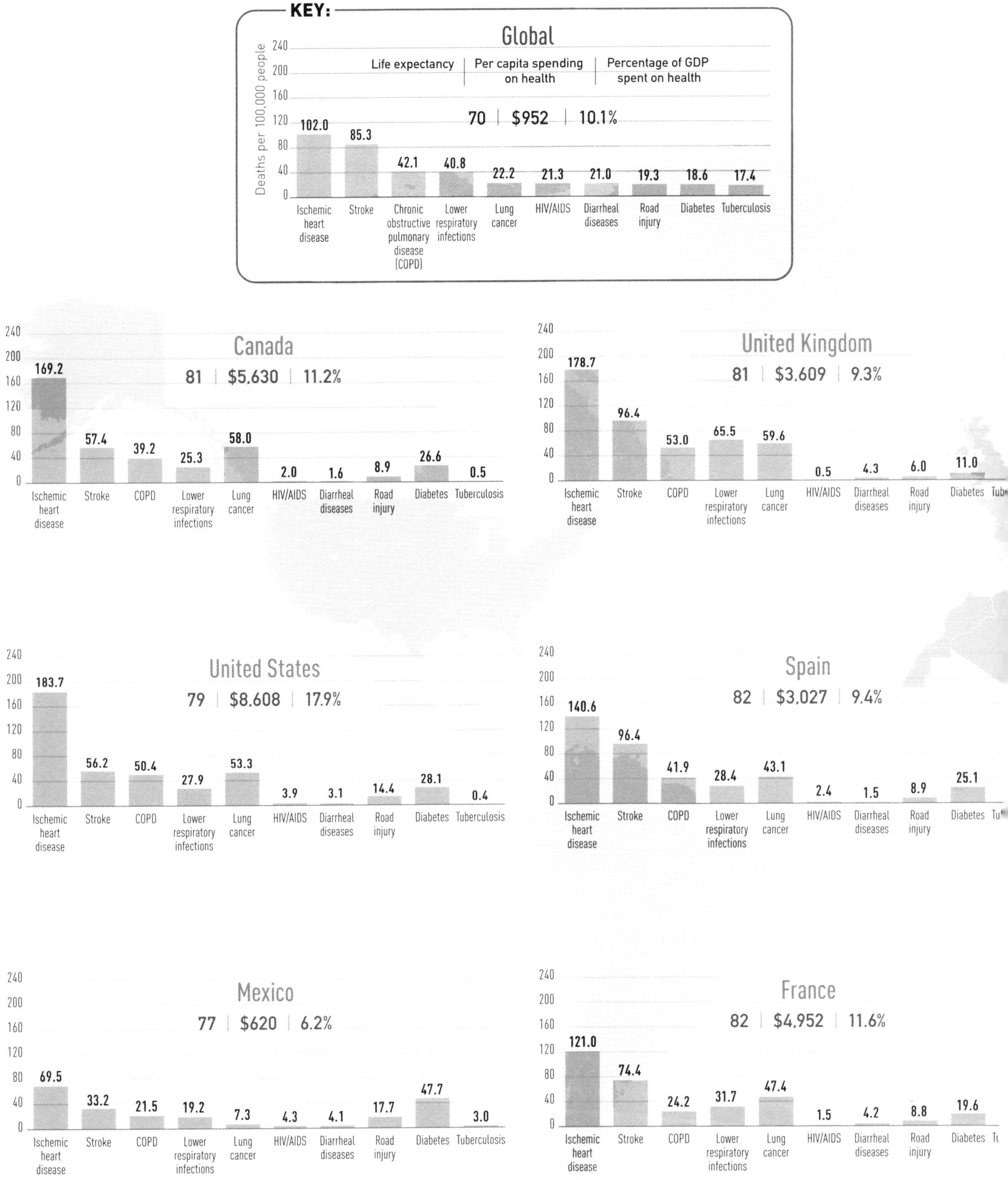

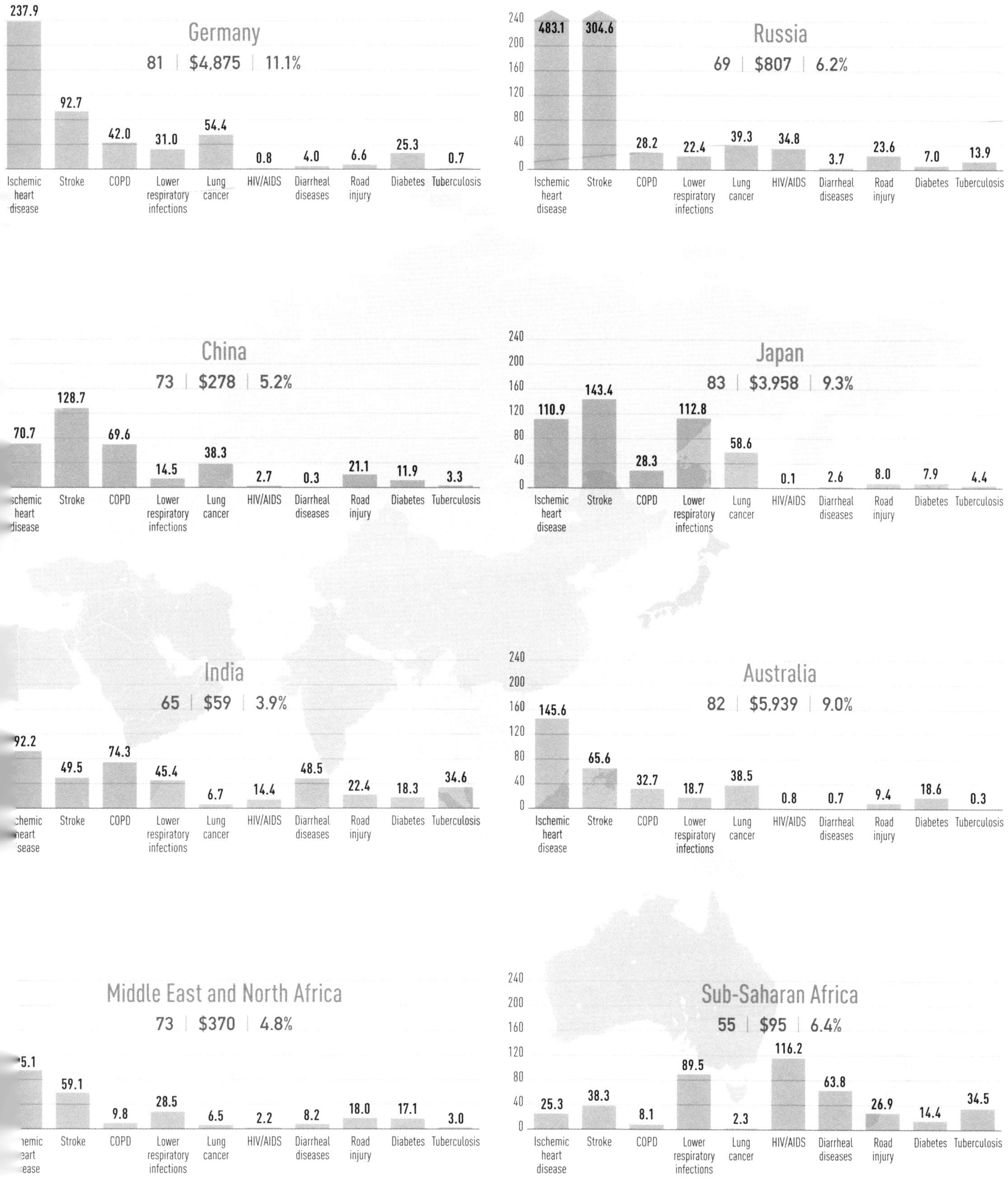

Sources: Data for deaths per 100,000 people are from the Institute for Health Metrics and Evaluation, University of Washington, "Global Burden of Disease," 2010. Data for life expectancy, per capita spending on health, and percentage of GDP spent on health are from World Bank Group, "World Development Indicators," 2013.

Key Global Health Statistics

Obesity

Source: World Health Organization, 2011.

Diabetes

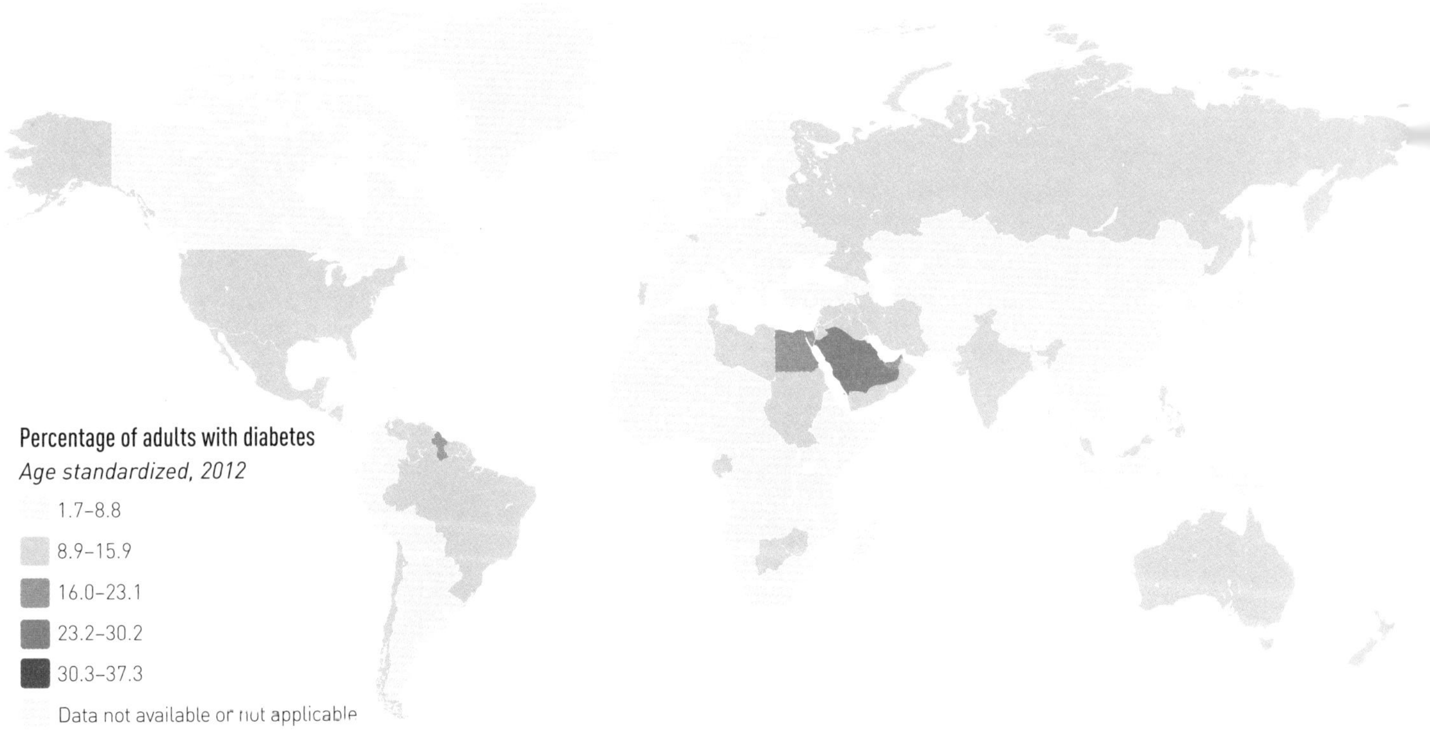

Source: International Diabetes Federation, *IDF Diabetes Atlas*, 5th edition (Brussels, Belgium: International Diabetes Federation, 2011).

eaths from Road Injury

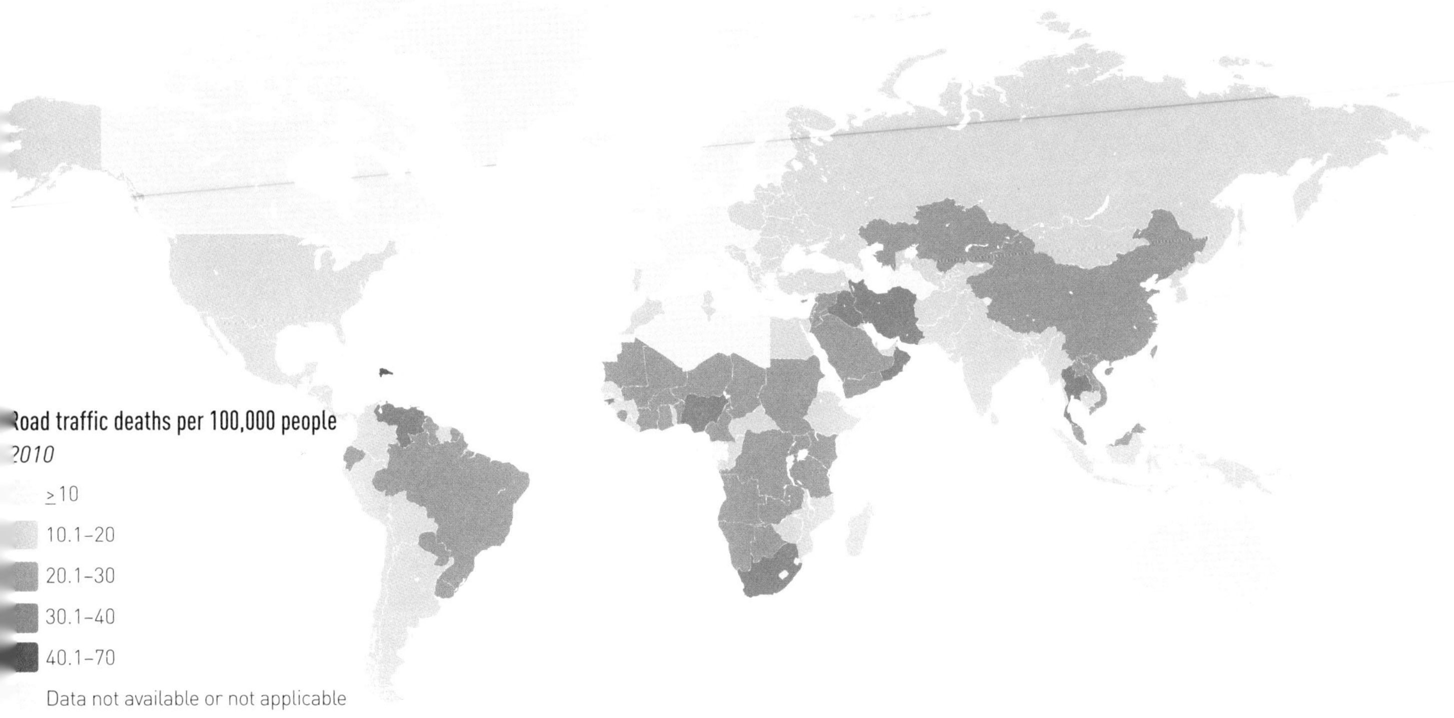

rce: World Health Organization, 2013.

inking Water

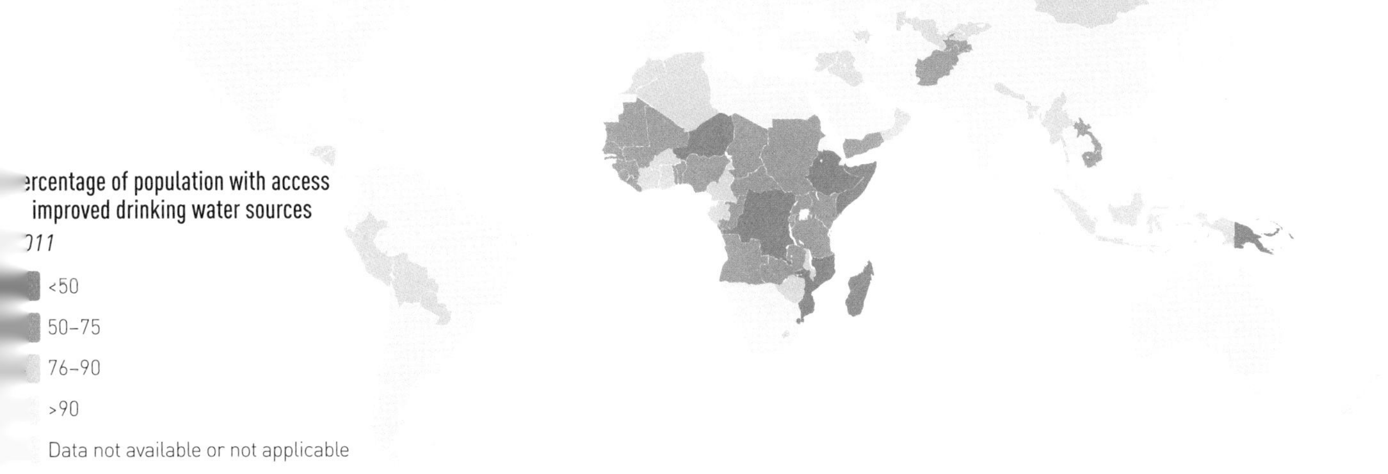

ce: World Health Organization, 2011.

Flooding in Hoboken, New Jersey, in the aftermath of Hurricane Sandy affected water supplies and other infrastructure.

Water/Sanitary Waste. Global freshwater demand is projected to increase by 55 percent between 2000 and 2050 as consumption by manufacturing industries, thermal power plants, and domestic use increases. Competing demands will put water use by farmers at risk. More than 240 million people globally will lack access to clean water by 2050, with 1.4 billion people needing basic sanitary waste systems.

Road Accidents. Road traffic injuries were the eighth leading cause of death in 2010 and are projected to become the fifth leading cause of death by 2030, with low- and middle-income countries bearing a greater burden. Though these countries account for approximately half of the world's vehicles, they make up over 90 percent of road fatalities.

Road injuries are the eighth leading cause of death globally. Investments in transportation should improve safety for drivers, pedestrians, and other users of road and transit networks.

A Path Forward

The built environment is part of the problem, but it can also be part of the solution.

To meet current health challenges, countries will need the following:

- Careful land planning and urban design;
- Infrastructure investments and expansions that provide safe, healthy, sustainable places for people;
- Greener buildings to provide healthier interiors and reduce the use of natural resources, such as energy and water;
- Safer streets and highways, and public transportation systems with infrastructure for walking, biking, and other active transportation modes;
- Healthier diets supported by local agriculture and better food supply and distribution systems; and
- Cleaner energy sources to combat increasing air pollution, and adequate supplies of clean water, especially in emerging countries.

INNOVATIONS IN HEALTH

Augustenborg EcoDistrict, Malmö, Sweden

The Augustenborg EcoDistrict is an urban community of 3,000 residents that was redeveloped in the late 1990s with green infrastructure, transportation options, and energy-saving measures. Together, these investments have enhanced both the environmental sustainability and health of residents.

Investments in Augustenborg included open space, increased waste recycling, and improved stormwater retention. New transportation options—including pedestrian and bike infrastructure, two electric trains, and a carpool system with electric vehicles and cars fueled by ethanol and biogas—added opportunities for active mobility and reduced energy use.

The project has helped boost local pride and civic engagement and launch new local businesses, generating jobs. EcoDistricts like Augustenborg show how communities can make intentional decisions to redevelop in healthier, more sustainable ways.

The open stormwater management system in the Augustenborg district of Malmö, Sweden, helps alleviate the city's flooding. (Scandinavian Green Roof Institute)

3 Better Health through Community Design

The High Line park on Manhattan's west side, which opened in 2009, was built on a historic freight rail line elevated above the streets. (Iwan Baan)

Designing a healthy community—with new development, redevelopment, or incremental infill—begins with an understanding of how community design contributes to health.

The Robert Wood Johnson Foundation notes that physical features, social relationships, and available services and opportunities within neighborhoods influence health in important ways, including by shaping choices and behaviors. Community wellness and safety are influenced by neighborhood factors, such as access to transportation, the condition of buildings, the presence and quality of sidewalks and places to play or exercise, and the density of convenience stores, liquor stores, and fast-food restaurants relative to grocery stores that sell fresh foods.

Comprehensive community planning presents an opportunity for planners, developers, and residents to address health through zoning ordinances, design guidelines, and capital improvements. Healthy community changes to comprehensive plans can be addressed through amendments, revised codes or ordinances, overlay health plans, and stand-alone health-promoting policies.

Healthy places are communities that are developed, designed, and built to promote good health.

—U.S. Centers for Disease Control and Prevention

PROJECTS THAT WORK FOR HEALTH

Mueller, Austin, Texas

Elements such as sidewalks, parks, open space, bike routes, and alleys, along with diverse uses and destinations, support more physical and social activity, according to preliminary results from a study of the health impacts of walkable communities. The study was conducted at Mueller, a community with a plan that received Silver certification under the U.S. Green Building Council's Leadership in Energy and Environmental Design for Neighborhood Development (LEED-ND) program.

With an estimated 13,000 residents and 13,000 employees at completion, Mueller is being redeveloped by Catellus Development Corporation in a joint project with the city of Austin on the site of the former Robert Mueller Municipal Airport.

The Texas A&M University study sponsored by the American Institute of Architects asked residents to compare their activity levels at Mueller with their previous activity levels. Nearly three out of four residents reported more physical activity, including an average of 48 additional minutes per week of walking and 90 minutes fewer per week of traveling in a car. Residents walked more on neighborhood sidewalks, in parks and on trails, and along greenways than they did in their previous neighborhood.

The Mueller development in Austin, Texas, includes a variety of trails, parks, pools, and sports courts to encourage residents to be physically active. (Thomas McConnell Photography)

Many Health Topics Are Included in Comprehensive Plans

Percentage of adopted U.S. comprehensive plans that address listed public health topic

Topic	Percentage	Includes
Active living	57%	Active transportation, physical activity, recreation
Environmental health	37%	Brownfields, clean air, clean water, environmental health, environmental justice, toxic exposures
Safety	36%	Injury prevention, public safety
Climate	34%	Climate change, emergency preparedness
Health care	19%	Aging, clinical services, healthy homes, health services, human services, mental health
Social health	13%	Social capital, social equity
Food and nutrition	9%	Food access, food safety, food security, healthy eating, nutrition
Chronic disease	7%	Chronic disease prevention, health disparities, obesity prevention

Source: American Planning Association.

Although entire new communities are being developed with a foundation of health-promoting design, incremental design through individual projects, such as infill housing, fresh-food markets, and mixed-use development next to transit stops, also contribute to healthier neighborhoods.

BY THE NUMBERS

Good Design and Opportunities for Health

23.5 million

Number of Americans who do not have access to a supermarket within one mile of home

16

Average daily increase in minutes of physical activity for children who walk or bike to school

72%

Percentage of U.S. baby boomers (ages 48–66) who would prefer a smaller home with a shorter commute over a larger home with a longer commute

10%–30%

Potential reduction in per capita vehicle travel from an integrated Complete Streets program

Sources: U.S. Department of Agriculture; Active Living Research; *ITE Journal*; Urban Land Institute.

Smart Growth: Building toward Health and Saving Money

A growing body of research suggests that evidence-based architectural and urban design strategies are building a foundation for healthier lives. Community design patterns and urban design elements that promote healthy living follow many of the principles of smart growth and sustainable development, as well as concepts related to design for active living.

Smart growth means building compact communities with housing and transportation choices near jobs, services, and schools to support local economies and to protect the environment. A vibrant local economy, a balance between jobs and housing that reduces the need for long commutes, and diversity in housing sizes, types, and costs, including adequate affordable housing, are all important to healthy and sustainable communities.

Smart growth development costs one-third less for upfront infrastructure, such as roads, sewers, and water lines. It saves an average of 10 percent on ongoing delivery of police, fire, and ambulance services and generates ten times more tax revenue per acre than conventional suburban development, according to a Smart Growth America survey of 17 studies of development scenarios.

Compact + Mixed Use + Transit

Compact, mixed-use, walkable development, a high degree of street connectivity, microscale urban design features, and links to transit are key factors of a walkable community, according to the U.S. Environmental Protection Agency (EPA). The cumulative

INNOVATIONS IN HEALTH

ULI's Ten Principles for Building Healthy Places

In August 2013, a group of interdisciplinary experts convened by ULI developed a set of principles for building healthy communities. These principles draw on insights gleaned during three Advisory Services panels conducted in Colorado in spring 2013, and are elaborated on in a separate ULI report, *Ten Principles for Building Healthy Places*.

1. Put people first.
2. Recognize the economic value.
3. Empower champions for health.
4. Energize shared spaces.
5. Make healthy choices easy.
6. Ensure equitable access.
7. Mix it up.
8. Embrace unique character.
9. Promote access to healthy food.
10. Make it active.

The Avenue, a mixed-use development near George Washington University in Washington, D.C., contains office, residential, and retail space, including a grocery store, a bank, and restaurants. (Kevin Weber)

PROJECTS THAT WORK FOR HEALTH

Mariposa, Denver, Colorado

The design for Mariposa, winner of the U.S. Environmental Protection Agency's National Smart Growth Achievement Award and a project of the Denver Housing Authority, is a holistic plan for redeveloping public housing that uses a health lens to achieve benefits for the community.

Begun in 2009, the project includes 900 homes—270 public housing units within a mix of income levels and housing types—on 15 acres next to a new light-rail station in Denver's La Alma/Lincoln Park neighborhood. Partners in the transit-oriented development project include the city of Denver and the Regional Transportation District.

The former South Lincoln Homes, built in 1953, typified the approach of concentrating the poor in social and economic isolation. The lack of education and jobs left the neighborhood stagnating with few options for upward economic mobility. The statistics on residents' health were alarming: 55 percent were overweight or obese, while more than 38 percent indicated a health condition that kept them from working.

The redevelopment plan by the housing authority and a team led by architecture firm Mithun focused on improving the physical health of residents and the financial health of the community. Residents identified their main health issues: the need to increase residents' physical activity; to improve pedestrian, bike, and traffic safety and access to health care; to reduce crime and the fear of crime; and to improve social cohesion.

The Mariposa team also customized San Francisco's Healthy Development Measurement Tool to assess the health conditions of residents and identify opportunities for improvement. It developed the Mariposa Healthy Living Initiative, aimed at integrating health into every aspect of the project's design, construction, and implementation.

Mariposa shows signs of early success. The Tapiz Apartments is a 100-unit LEED Platinum building with a community center that offers job training, health and wellness programs, social activities, and art classes. A state-of-the-art kitchen and café house a culinary academy that prepares youth for jobs in the food industry. Residents can grow their own fresh foods in community gardens managed by Denver Urban Gardens.

Four newer buildings with 93 apartments built to LEED Gold standards feature green elements like rooftop solar panels. The $22 million construction created 300 jobs and generated $47 million for the local economy.

Mariposa, a project of the Denver Housing Authority, includes 900 homes, adjacent transit access, a community center, and community gardens. (Rachel MacCleery)

effect of smaller-scale infill development and development near transit stations can be a catalyst for other land use changes that benefit public health and the environment.

Neighborhoods with destinations that people can walk or bike to have been shown to support a healthy lifestyle. A grid pattern, for example, maximizes opportunities for walking. Even mundane routines like walking to the grocery store provide opportunities for exercise and chance encounters with friends and neighbors.

"Walk scores" used to market real estate in 3,000 cities in the United States, Canada, and Australia are attracting millennials and baby boomers to urban neighborhoods. Walk Score is an online, geographic information system–based tool that assesses neighborhood walkability. Ranging from zero to 100, walk scores of 70 or higher indicate neighborhoods where people can live without a car.

Houses with above-average walkability command a premium of about $4,000 to $34,000 more than houses with average walkability in typical metropolitan areas, according to CEOs for Cities.

The Power of Parks and Trails

Design for active living aims to get people moving to improve health and well-being. Regular physical exercise helps control weight and reduces the risks of cardiovascular diseases, type 2 diabetes, and some cancers. It also strengthens bones and muscles, boosts immunity and balance, and increases the chances of living longer. Exercise has been shown to relieve stress, anxiety, and mild depression.

Research shows that living near parks and recreation facilities leads to higher levels of physical activity. A study from the *Journal*

INNOVATIONS IN HEALTH

Being Intentional about Health Outcomes

Tools such as the Health Impact Assessment (HIA) and the Healthy Development Measurement Tool (HDMT) are used to quantify and qualify the public health impacts of proposed policies, plans, or development projects.

Health Impact Assessments help communities assess the potential effects of a proposed policy, plan, program, or project on community health, including the distribution of benefits and costs within the community. HIAs recommend strategies for monitoring and managing health and bring public health issues to decision makers outside of the public health field, such as in transportation and land use. HIAs can be voluntary or regulatory processes that focus on health outcomes.

The Healthy Development Measurement Tool is an evaluation instrument used to assess and address health needs in urban development plans and projects with the goal of achieving a higher-quality social and physical environment that advances good health. Created by the San Francisco Department of Public Health, the HDMT has six core objectives: environmental stewardship, sustainable and safe transportation, social cohesion, public infrastructure, adequate and healthy housing, and a healthy economy.

INNOVATIONS IN HEALTH

Blue Zones Project, Albert Lea, Minnesota

Albert Lea, a statistically average U.S. city of 18,000 located 90 miles south of Minneapolis, underwent an extraordinary transformation in 2009 through the Blue Zones Vitality Project, based on Dan Buettner's book *The Blue Zones*, which is about five areas around the world where people live up to 12 years longer than the average American.

Albert Lea residents adopted lifestyle and environmental changes, such as adding workplace wellness policies, revising restaurant menus and vending machine offerings, and establishing community gardens, walking clubs, walking school buses, and hiking trails. Residents' well-being improved in four areas: they ate healthier, became more active, connected with one another, and found a greater sense of purpose.

The research showed that the average life expectancy for Albert Lea's residents increased over three years, and participants lost a collective 12,000 pounds. Employers experienced an average 21 percent drop in absenteeism, and city employees showed a 40 percent decrease in health care costs.

BY THE NUMBERS

The Value of Proximity to Parks

$2,262

Estimated sales price premium for homes located near parks

$4 billion

Amount of private investment and development spurred by New York City's High Line project

103%

Increase in value for properties within a five-minute walk of the High Line from 2003 (before construction) to 2011

68%

Percentage of U.S. millennials (ages 18–34) who cite proximity to parks as an important community characteristic

Sources: Active Living Research; *New York Times*/City of New York City; New York City Economic Development Corporation; Urban Land Institute.

The Gansevoort Woodland section of the High Line in Manhattan is one of several distinct "neighborhoods" that make up the elevated park. (Iwan Baan)

A parklet in San Francisco's North Beach neighborhood, designed by Rebar, provides a gathering place and seating for the adjacent pizzeria. (Søren Jensen/Rebar Group Inc.)

of Applied Physiology found that communities designed for exercise can prevent 90 percent of type 2 diabetes, as well as 50 percent of heart disease, stroke, and site-specific cancers.

Communities designed for active living feature public places such as greenways, multiuse trails, playgrounds, pools, athletic fields, and other recreation facilities that encourage physical exercise.

Programming these public spaces with activities such as family "fun runs," healthy living festivals, and free yoga classes can support a culture of healthy active living.

Civic and cultural places for people to gather—such as plazas, libraries, and theaters—are important for social and mental health, for a sense of community belonging, and as a focus for urban development.

Dozens of studies show that parks spur economic development by attracting homebuyers and boosting residential property values.

Manhattan's High Line, the 20-block-long park constructed on a former elevated freight rail line, has become a worldwide sensation, bringing over 3.7 million visitors to the city in 2011. A study by the New York City Economic Development Corporation showed that property values near the park increased 103 percent between 2003 and 2011.

Parklets—small temporary parks constructed by extending platforms from sidewalks into driving lanes or parking zones and adding seating, landscaping, art, and bike parking—are creating livelier streets.

San Francisco, which started the first formal parklets in 2010, now has 38 developed and maintained by community organizations, local businesses, and residents. These "outdoor living rooms" also draw patrons to retail shops and cafés.

The award-winning Milwaukee Riverwalk reinvigorated a moribund two-mile river corridor in the heart of Milwaukee's business district with new plazas, parks, walkways, and public art. As of 2002, the $12 million Riverwalk had attracted over $700 million in private investment in new restaurants, cafés, shops, offices, and boating facilities along the cleaned-up river and had drawn 3,500 new downtown residents to riverfront condominiums redeveloped from warehouses.

Aging in Place: It Never Gets Old

Aging in place is a concept of providing infrastructure, services, and opportunities that allow people to live independently in their homes as they age.

The majority of people over 50 want to stay in their own homes as long as possible, according to a survey by AARP (formerly the American Association of Retired Persons).

The Milwaukee Riverwalk project increased public access to the water and spurred residential redevelopment of nearby warehouses. (©KenKay Associates)

Communities that are walkable and connected with safe level sidewalks, well-marked crosswalks, and adequate lighting will serve people as they age, especially when they have limited mobility and can no longer drive. Elements such as accessible housing, frequent transit service, nearby grocery stores and health care facilities, and gathering places support healthy and active lifestyles for seniors.

Most Older Americans Do Not Want to Move

Percentage of Americans who want to remain in their current home for as long as possible, by age group

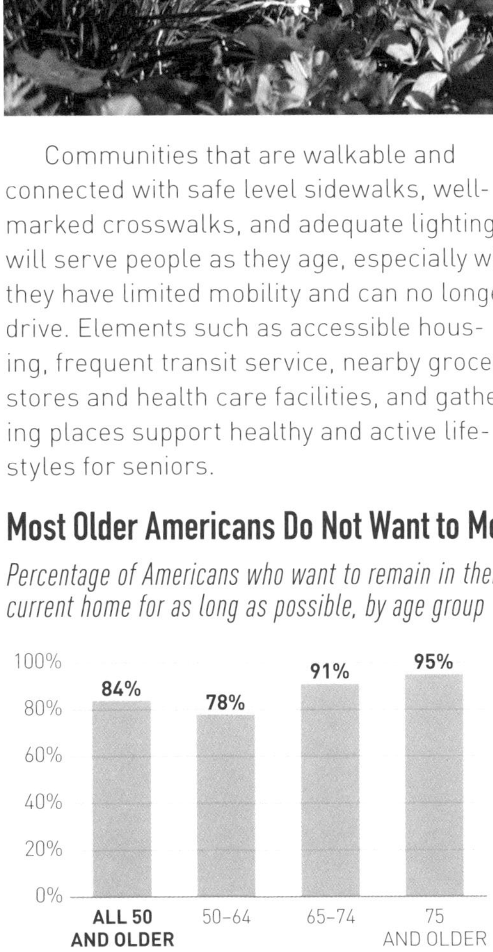

Source: AARP.

Playgrounds at schools provide opportunities for play and recreation during and after the school day. (Rachel MacCleery)

In some communities, volunteer networks provide services that allow seniors to remain in their homes.

For seniors who want to downsize or are living on limited incomes, supportive housing options include senior group homes and cooperatives and accessory dwelling units, or apartments attached to homes or located above garages.

School's (Too Far) Out

Suburban building codes in many U.S. communities have led to large K–12 school campuses located miles from residential neighborhoods. Such schools create challenges to students' ability to walk and bike to school and require that they be driven or bused.

The lack of sidewalks, crosswalks, and bike lanes in many communities prevent safe walking or biking to school. Amenities like bike lanes and trails connecting to schools, bike racks, and programs that reward kids for walking, biking, or busing to school every day have also been successful in getting kids moving.

Many schools in the United States have begun Safe Routes to School programs to create safe and easy ways for children to walk or bike to school. In 2012, the state of California authorized the use of Safe Routes to School funding for programs in rural communities, including safer access to school bus stops.

There Are Many Ways to Increase the Amount of Activity Children Get Each Day

Minutes of physical activity gained per day per child from various improvements and activities

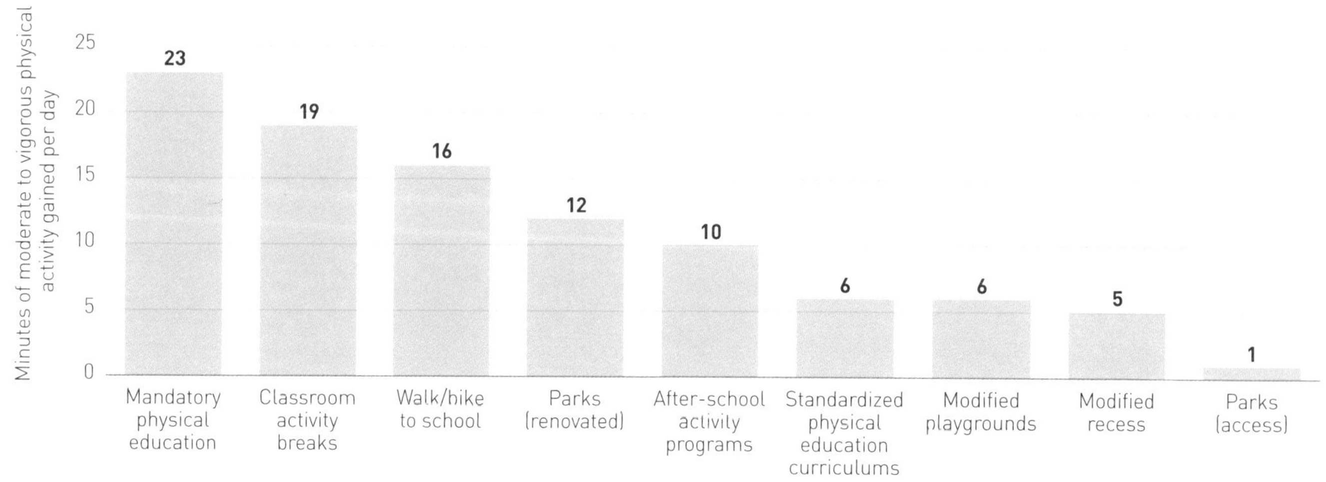

Source: Active Living Research.

INSIGHTS FROM THE EXPERTS

Dr. Richard Jackson, Chair, Department of Environmental Health Sciences, University of California, Los Angeles

Richard Jackson, MD, MPH, FAAP, is a pediatrician and chair of the University of California, Los Angeles Department of Environmental Health Sciences. In 2013, he was a fellow at Hunters College. Dr. Jackson was formerly director of the National Center for Environmental Health of the Centers for Disease Control and Prevention and hosted the 2012 public television series *Designing Healthy Communities*.

Q: *What are the greatest health threats contained in our built environment?*

A: Chronic diseases. A generation ago, 50 percent of American men were getting daily exercise, and now it's only 17 percent. Walking to the store or the train is just as good as being on a treadmill in a fitness club. If you're in an attractive safe place, that's conducive to walking. Frederick Law Olmsted saw parks and trails as a necessity for health; he called parks the lungs of the city. Now we have science that supports that—air quality is better and cooler in parks.

Q: *What concerns you most about the health of children in our car-centered society?*

A: The average 11-year-old is 11 pounds heavier than a generation ago. Only one in eight kids now walks or bikes to school. Kids are increasingly car dependent, especially growing up in the suburbs, and many aren't developing autonomy and independence. Every child in America should be able to walk or bike to school. We need to build good sidewalks and bikeways with adults on them to help kids feel safe and provide eyes on the street. The more people are out engaged in the world, the safer we'll all be.

Q: *What are some of the key built-environment elements you recommend to make communities healthier?*

A: Neighborhoods that put people first, rather than cars. Put infrastructure in place that supports walking, biking, and car sharing. We can't fix the world by fixing the built environment, but it's important that our environment not place impediments to our well-being. The built environment can help us be healthier.

Q: *You've said we need to make beautiful places that attract people to walk around and interact socially.*

A: Numerous studies show that children who have increased physical activity can better manage diseases like attention deficit disorder and depression. I want architects, designers, developers, and planners to understand that health is a lot more than the absence of disease—it's well-being. Look at where people live long in the world, and you see 80-year-olds out walking and working. Well-being is partly diet, but it's also physical activity.

Q: *Do you have other advice for designing and developing healthy places?*

A: We have a window of opportunity, where we can make changes that are good for the planet, our children, and our grandchildren, as well as our economy. We need more evidence of new development and how it affects people's health, to attract people to those places. Many ULI members are doing brownfield or greenfield development as a return on investment. I'd like to see a return on investment in social, cultural, and human health terms. So many of our investments are built on short-term return, but we have to look at the long-term effects.

Put infrastructure in place that supports walking, biking, and car sharing. . . . The built environment can help us be healthier. **—Dr. Richard Jackson**

CHAPTER 4

Active Transportation

City workers walk and bike over Waterloo Bridge in London during the evening commute.

Transportation infrastructure determines people's options for getting around to meet their daily needs. Mobility and travel decisions affect human health and the natural environment by affecting physical activity levels, air and water quality, development patterns, and global climate conditions. Worldwide, transportation is responsible for 25 to 70 percent of urban outdoor air pollution, depending on the city.

Automobile transportation and the lack of safe infrastructure were also at least partially responsible for 1.24 million roadway deaths and 20 to 50 million nonfatal injuries in 2010. Over one-quarter of those killed in that year were pedestrians and cyclists. After seven years of decline, traffic deaths in the United States rose in 2012 to 36,200. Many road accidents occur in the developing world, where investments in safe road infrastructure and public transit are especially needed.

In the United States and other countries, shifting demographics, household finances, and lifestyles, as well as a continuing outward growth of cities and towns, for decades have increased vehicle miles traveled (VMT).

In the United States, cars are still the primary transportation mode; more than 80 percent of U.S. workers drive or ride in a car to work. But although total driving has continued to increase in the United States, per capita driving has declined every year

BY THE NUMBERS

Transportation Deaths and Injuries

200% Increased likelihood of accidents involving pedestrians on roadways without sidewalks compared with roadways with sidewalks on both sides

47,700 Number of U.S. pedestrians killed from 2000 to 2009

1 in 4 Share of global road traffic deaths accounted for by pedestrians and bicyclists

15% Reduction in number of automobile accidents involving pedestrian injuries after installation of traffic-calming elements

Sources: Federal Highway Administration; Transportation for America; World Health Organization; Active Living Research.

INNOVATIONS IN HEALTH

International Development Banks: $175 Billion for Active Transportation

Multilateral development banks (MDBs), which provide financing for infrastructure investments in developing countries, are changing their approach to transportation lending. Past MDB policies have encouraged the construction of highways and roads, helping to fuel growth in private vehicles and a rise in transport-related energy use in the developing world.

At the June 2012 United Nations Sustainable Development Conference in Rio de Janeiro, the world's largest MDBs, including the World Bank, Asian Development Bank, and Inter-American Development Bank, committed to providing more than $175 billion over ten years to support sustainable transport, shifting investments away from auto-oriented transportation and toward transit and other active options.

Efficient transport of people and goods and access to environmentally sustainable, safe, and affordable transportation are "a means to improve social equity, health, resilience of cities, urban-rural linkages and productivity of rural areas," noted the MDBs.

More than 80 percent of U.S. workers commute in vehicles, though public transit ridership has been increasing year by year.

since 2004, while public transit rides have increased every year, reaching 10.5 billion in 2012, according to the American Public Transportation Association (APTA).

In developing countries like China and India, however, car sales and VMT are in the fast lane. To continue to reduce VMT in developed countries and reverse it in developing countries, communities need to provide more active and public transportation options.

Public and private investments in transportation infrastructure and operations amount to over $57 billion annually in the United States, according to APTA, with most of it dedicated to building highways and improving road infrastructure. As demand increases for public and active transportation options, funding priorities worldwide are beginning to shift to support healthier options, such as walking, biking, and public transit.

Transportation That Gets Us Moving

A growing body of research shows that a safe, accessible, affordable, and well-built transportation network with a range of alternatives can enhance community health and well-being. Residents of mixed-use livable communities with transit options weigh less, are more physically active, and experience less chronic disease.

Investments in the built environment that promote active living, such as public transit, sidewalks, bike lanes, multiuse trails, and other alternative transportation infrastructure, have been shown to reduce health care costs and enhance local economies.

Universal design approaches encourage accessible transportation use for seniors and people with disabilities. The design principles promote barrier-free and independent access through such elements as curb cuts, transit ticket machines accessible for wheelchair users, and buses equipped with ramps rather than onboard lifts.

Walking

Walking, the most common form of exercise for most people, helps reduce weight, maintain cardiovascular fitness, strengthen bones and muscles, and improve cognitive brain function. When trips are within one mile, 40 percent of people walk to work, school, shopping, and other destinations. Twenty minutes of walking, especially repeated during the day, can help maintain a healthy weight and fitness level.

Mixed-use neighborhoods with connected streets encourage people to walk. Well-marked crosswalks, pedestrian-activated

BY THE NUMBERS

Opportunities for Biking and Walking

34 Number of active U.S. bike-share programs in 2013

64% Increase in U.S. bike commuters from 1990 to 2009

76% Percentage of U.S. millennials (ages 18–34) who cite walkability as an important community characteristic

44% Percentage of U.S. adults who say they walk to a destination daily or weekly

Sources: Earth Policy Institute; University Transportation Research Center; Urban Land Institute.

INNOVATIONS IN HEALTH

Active Design Guidelines for Communities

New York City has developed a set of Active Design Guidelines for communities, which outline priorities for changes in the built environment to promote physical activity. Several of the city's departments, in collaboration with the New York chapter of the American Institute of Architects and academic leaders in architecture and planning, developed the guidelines in 2010.

The guidelines include the following:

- **Mixed land use.** Develop and maintain mixed land use in city neighborhoods.
- **Transit.** Improve access to transit and transit facilities.
- **Parks and active space.** Improve access to plazas, parks, open spaces, and recreational facilities, and design these spaces for active use.
- **Food.** Improve access to full-service grocery stores and fresh produce.
- **Street design.** Design accessible, pedestrian-friendly streets with high connectivity, traffic-calming features, landscaping, lighting, benches, and water fountains.
- **Bicycling.** Encourage bicycling for recreation and transportation by developing continuous bicycle networks and incorporating infrastructure like safe indoor and outdoor bicycle parking.

Safe pedestrian infrastructure includes elements such as wide sidewalks, crosswalks, traffic crossing signals, and adequate lighting. (Rachel MacCleery)

traffic signals, wide sidewalks, and adequate streetlighting create a safer, more pleasant environment for walking. Buildings close to sidewalks, attractive routes with shade trees or canopies, interesting architecture, and other elements also make walking more appealing.

PROJECTS THAT WORK FOR HEALTH

The Uptown, Oakland, California

The Uptown, a LEED Silver 700-home apartment community developed by Forest City Enterprises on a four-city-block brownfield, anchors the new Uptown District in Oakland. A city park is located within a network of interior courtyards that buffers noise; allows access to views, light, and greenery; and enhances livability.

New street standards provide a walkable environment with narrow roadways, wide sidewalks, and shade trees. Safe and attractive routes connect to the nearby civic center, transit station, and cafés, shops, and cinema.

Fox Square Park, part of the Uptown apartment community in Oakland, California, is open to the public and features programming that includes a public art installation. (Forest City Enterprises Inc.)

Wheeling and Dealing

Bicycling is the fastest-growing form of transportation in the United States. Most noncommute trips are less than three miles in length, which means many of these trips could be shifted to bikes if infrastructure and facilities were available.

Millennials are moving to cities and compact suburbs where the bike infrastructure and culture support their lifestyle choices to get around by pedaling and reduce car ownership.

New York City, which has created a 280-mile network of bicycle lanes since 2007, has had 40 percent fewer fatal accidents on streets with bike lanes. Streets with "protected" bike lanes separated by parked cars are up to 50 percent safer for everyone.

Investments that promote biking include separated or well-marked bike lanes and multiuse trails that link to transit; bike racks located at transit stops, schools, and other public places; bike maintenance facilities; and buses and other transit modes that can carry bikes.

The Santa Monica, California, Bike Center, designed by Brooks+Scarpa and built in two locations, offers showers, lockers, bike storage, rentals, tours, retail, and a repair shop as part of municipal garage improvements. The Bike Center has increased downtown biking by residents and visitors and has provided over $100,000 in city revenue within two years of its opening.

As part of the global bike revolution, bike shares—networks of public or commercial bicycles available for short trips—are proliferating in more than 500 cities in 49 countries, says the Earth Policy Institute. Started in

INNOVATIONS IN HEALTH

Protected Two-Way Bike Lanes in Chicago, Illinois

Downtown Chicago's Dearborn Avenue in the Central Loop district was reconfigured in December 2012 to provide a two-way bike lane protected by a parking lane and bollards. A study of the bike lanes' first six months proved that they provided a safer environment for cyclists and pedestrians, with reduced vehicle speeds and conflicts with drivers.

From 2006 to 2011, there were 1,140 reported crashes on the 1.15-mile section of Dearborn, with pedestrians and bicyclists involved in more than half of the accidents that included injuries. Since the project was completed, no reports of crashes between cyclists and vehicles or cyclists and pedestrians have been reported. Bike traffic has increased with the $450,000 project, which removed a vehicle lane.

(John Greenfield)

Obesity Rates Are Lower in Countries Where Lots of People Bike and Walk to Work

Levels of bicycling and walking to work versus measured obesity levels for selected countries

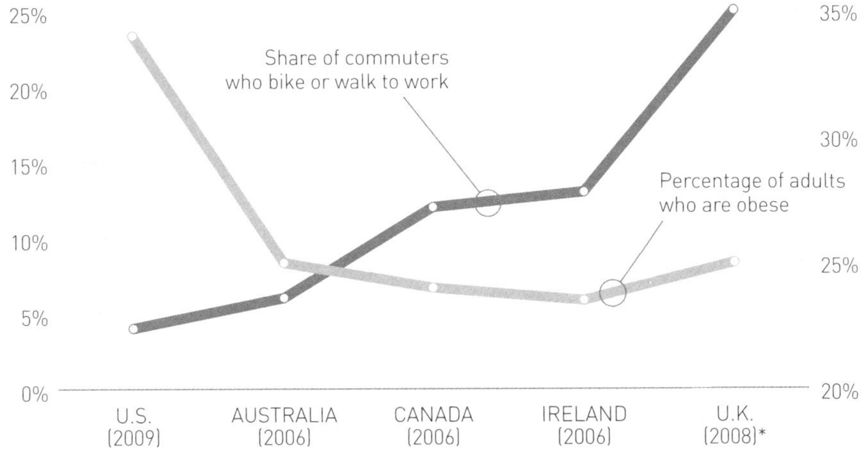

Sources: *Built Environment* journal; the Organization for Economic Cooperation and Development.
*U.K. data are for all trips, not just work trips.

INNOVATIONS IN HEALTH

Biking in Copenhagen, Portland, and Hangzhou

Biking is increasing in popularity as people recognize its multiple benefits. Cities across the globe are successfully implementing bike amenities and infrastructure to meet increasing demand.

Copenhagen Bike Superhighways. Copenhagen is recognized as one of the premier bike cities in the world. Good conditions for biking are part of the city's official health policy. In 2012, bikes were used for 36 percent of trips in the city. The city has increased biking's mode share and decreased travel time by improving connections between public transit and biking facilities, and by building bike "superhighways," contiguous standardized bike routes from other jurisdictions into the capital across distances of up to 14 miles.

Portland Bike Infrastructure. Portland, Oregon, boasts North America's best bike infrastructure system, with an investment in over 300 miles of bike lanes, bike boulevards, and off-street paths, which has launched an explosion in bike use. Between 1990 and 2008, bicycle use expanded 400 percent, whereas transit use increased 18 percent and driving declined 4 percent. The network's $60 million replacement value is equivalent to the construction costs of one mile of urban freeway.

Hangzhou Bike Share. Hangzhou's bike-share system is one of the largest in the world, with nearly 70,000 bikes. The city of 6.8 million incorporated a bike-share program into the public transportation system to increase transit ridership and solve the "last mile" issue between transit stations and riders' destinations. Started in 2008 with 61 stations and 2,800 bikes, the program has helped increase bike ridership to 38 percent of trips. Daily usage now averages 240,000 trips. Hangzhou public officials expect the bike-share system to expand to 175,000 bikes by 2020.

Nørrebrogade in Copenhagen, Denmark, known as the busiest bike street in the Western world, has been permanently closed to cars. (John Greenfield)

Global Bike Sharing Has Increased Dramatically since 2007

Number of bicycles in bike-sharing programs by region

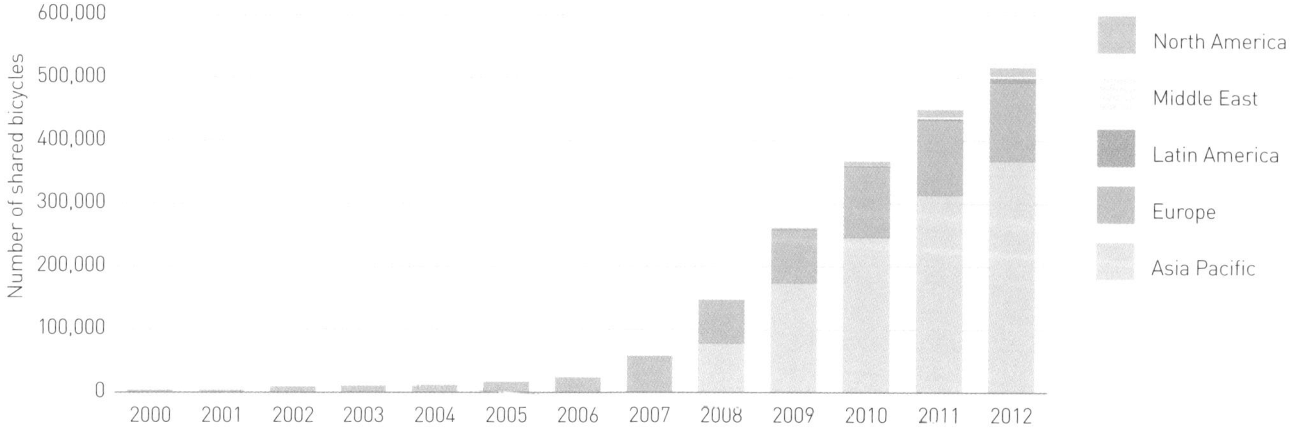

Source: Earth Policy Institute.

Amsterdam nearly 50 years ago, bike-share programs enhance mobility, alleviate traffic congestion, reduce air pollution, support local businesses, and attract more young people.

Transit Really Is Good for You

The steady growth of public transit in the United States indicates that people want to live and work in places where transit is an option. Studies show that people who are active tend to choose transit-accessible urban neighborhoods.

Transit users tend to be healthier and weigh less. A study of transit riders in Charlotte, North Carolina, found they were 81 percent less likely to be obese than those who drove to work from the same neighborhoods, according to the *American Journal of Preventative Medicine*. The study of Lynx light-rail riders showed they lost weight and body mass consistent with adding 1.2 miles of walking to their daily routine.

Transit investments are also economic development engines. In the Denver metropolitan region, where the $7.4 billion FasTracks public transit program is under construction, every public dollar invested generates $4 in local economic development over 20 years and creates over 6,200 jobs per year, according to the Regional Transportation District.

In the United States, all varieties of public transportation modes—heavy rail, light rail, buses, trolleys, streetcars, ferryboats, and vanpools—show increased ridership, according to APTA. What matters to riders are convenient high-quality transit options with frequent service, rather than particular modes.

Light-rail systems in the United States, including streetcars and trolleys, saw a 4.5 percent increase in ridership in 2012.

The bus rapid transit corridor system in Guangzhou, China, which opened in early 2010, is integrated with the city's bicycle and subway infrastructure. (Karl Fjellstrom/ITDP)

Within two years, 22 U.S. cities may have new streetcar systems, reports Clean Technica. The Tucson Modern Streetcar, a 3.9-mile line, will carry 3,600 riders daily on a route connecting downtown to the University of Arizona.

Bus rapid transit (BRT) combines the efficiency and user-friendliness of light rail with the economy and flexibility of on-road vehicles. Today, 63 BRT systems operate on six continents, and as many as 93 more are planned worldwide. Using high-speed buses that travel in dedicated lanes, BRT typically features efficient passenger boarding, adaptable routes, comfortable stations, and technology that updates travelers on bus locations and timing.

Lively streets and dense mixed uses located next to key transit stops encourage people to walk or bike to transit, and so do strategies such as placing building entrances near public transit stops along well-connected streets. Shelters and benches at transit stops also promote use, along with signage and maps that show routes, distances, and schedules.

Complete Streets Provide Safe Accommodations for All

Diagram of complete street example

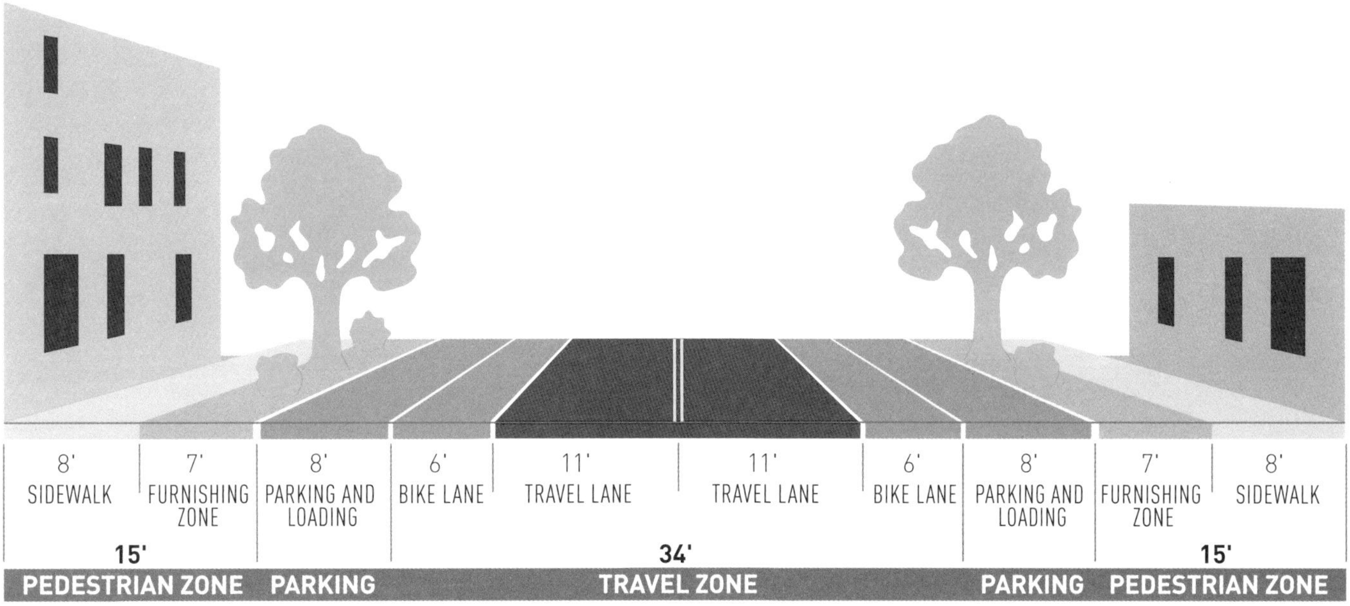

Source: SERA Architects.

Complete Streets: A Safe Bet

Traffic calming creates safer environments for pedestrians and cyclists, as well as drivers. Cities are increasingly using Complete Streets traffic-calming concepts, such as roundabouts and speed bumps, and narrowing traffic lanes through densely settled areas to slow and manage traffic.

In 2013, 500 U.S. communities have adopted Complete Streets policies designed to make streets safer and more accessible for all users. Complete Streets vary by community, but they often include sidewalks, bike lanes or wide paved shoulders, special bus lanes, accessible transit stops, frequent and safe crossing opportunities, and accessible pedestrian and cyclist signals.

Shared Cars and Car-Free Zones

Car-share programs are filling the gap for bike- and transit-using urbanites who don't want to own a car, or need one only for brief specific trips. Fewer cars on the road support the pursuit of shared economies and environmental protection by reducing private vehicle congestion and emissions.

Car-share programs have existed in Europe for decades and are catching on in the United States and elsewhere. Car2Go's 400,000 members worldwide are cruising in Smart cars in 23 cities.

Vauban, a neighborhood in Freiburg, Germany, was built for sustainability and features completely car-free streets, with a tram connecting to the town center. As of

The Car2Go car-share program, launched in 2008 in Ulm, Germany, is available in nine U.S. cities. (Sara Hammerschmidt)

2009, 70 percent of Vauban families did not own a car; those that did could rent parking outside the neighborhood.

Freiburg also has an excellent public transit system, anchored by an expanding web of tram routes and feeder buses. Residents can connect with frequent and fast long-distance trains to major cities in Germany and Europe.

Slimming Down Parking

As part of an active transportation and land use strategy, parking can be managed to encourage modes other than cars. Parking requirements can be reduced in transit-friendly areas, for example. Shared parking and shared cars help reduce space needs.

PROJECTS THAT WORK FOR HEALTH

HGST Campus, San Jose, California

The HGST (formerly Hitachi Global Storage Technologies Inc.) campus in San Jose is being transformed from a suburban-style business campus into a compact urban transit village with new offices, retail shops, services, and 3,000 homes.

The campus was under construction in 2013. The master plan, which was developed by San Francisco–based KenKay Associates, features a network of new public streets, plazas, open spaces, and parks with pedestrian and bicycle connections to two transit stations.

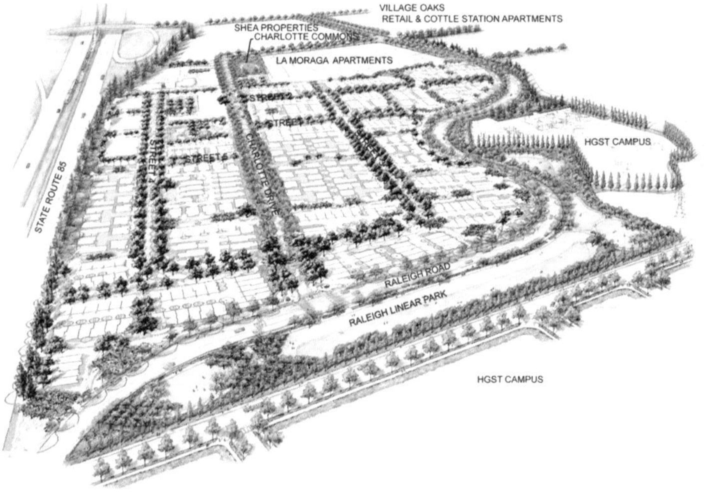

A rendering of the HGST transit village in San Jose, California, depicts a 400-acre walkable, bikeable, and transit-rich campus. (©KenKay Associates)

Technology and pricing strategies can also change the parking equation. Parking can generate revenues for other modes and needs through fees.

Efforts to reduce driving and lower development costs have led San Francisco and other cities to push for reduced parking in new development.

In Portland, Oregon, more than 100 parking spaces have been removed in storefront commercial districts, at the request of adjacent business owners and associations, to make room for 1,000 bicycle parking spaces at 64 locations.

Most streets in the Vauban district near Freiburg, Germany, are off-limits to automobiles, giving priority to other users. (Francis DEMANGE/Getty Images)

BY THE NUMBERS

Returns from Active Transportation

10% Estimated price premium for homes located near bike paths

$34,000 Average increase in value for homes located in areas with above-average walkability or bikeability compared with similar homes in areas with average walkability or bikeability

12 Number of bikes that can fit in one car parking space

51% Percentage of U.S. adults who prefer to live in a community with public transportation options

Sources: League of American Bicyclists; CEOs for Cities; DC Streetsblog; Urban Land Institute.

Bicycle facilities like this rack in Portland, Oregon, make it easier and more convenient for people to bike, and reduce the need for car parking.

5

Healthy Buildings, Healthy People

An accessible ramp at the Ed Roberts Campus, a transit-oriented development using universal design in Berkeley, California, provides an attractive alternative to an elevator. (Tim Griffith)

People spend 90 percent of their time indoors, at home or at work. Healthy buildings provide a foundation for healthy lives through design and construction that support well-being with safe, well-lit, attractive, comfortable, and pollution-free spaces.

Three-quarters of the U.S. building stock will be new or renovated over the next 30 years, according to Architecture 2030, a nonprofit organization dedicated to reducing climate-damaging greenhouse gas emissions by changing the way buildings and developments are planned, designed, and constructed. This forecast presents a great opportunity for the architecture and building communities to ensure that new and renovated buildings are designed to conserve energy, improve health, and encourage healthy behaviors.

Many buildings worldwide were constructed under substandard conditions or are in need of repairs to maintain their safety and livability. Toxic building materials and finishes—from cabinetry made of certain pressed-wood products to asbestos-containing insulation—are a source of indoor air pollution that can cause asthma and other serious respiratory problems. Buildings in many parts of the world contain "red list" hazardous substances, such as mercury, polyvinyl chloride, formaldehyde, and lead.

Indoor air pollution can cause health problems ranging from coughs, eye irritation, headaches, and allergic reactions to potentially life-threatening conditions, such as carbon monoxide poisoning. Health threats from "sick buildings" contaminated by mold or bacteria can make occupants ill, reduce employee productivity through absenteeism, and reduce real estate values.

Buildings are also responsible for a large share of the world's energy use. Since 1950, the U.S. population has doubled, but building energy use has quadrupled. Energy use has grown steadily for both the residential and commercial sectors since the 1950s, though home use has varied more because of weather, income, and economic activity.

BY THE NUMBERS

Building Design

8.5% Reduction in number of recovery days for hospital patients with views of nature

75% Average reduction in use of artificial lighting in buildings with well-designed daylighting schemes

3/1,500 Average number of additional miles walked/calories burned per month by a person taking the stairs rather than an elevator or escalator

90% Average share of time Americans spend indoors, where pollutant concentrations can be two to five times greater than those outside due to ventilation and building materials

Sources: *Science* magazine; *Energy and Buildings* journal; *Medicine & Science in Sports & Exercise* journal; U.S. Environmental Protection Agency.

INNOVATIONS IN HEALTH

Global Programs for Sustainable and Healthy Buildings and Communities

Some well-established global programs for rating and certifying buildings, such as BREEAM and LEED, focus on energy efficiency and sustainability and also address some aspects of health, such as using nontoxic building materials and ensuring healthy indoor air quality:

Building Research Establishment Environmental Assessment Method (BREEAM). BREEAM is the world's most popular environmental assessment and rating system, with more than 250,000 buildings certified since 1990. Based in the United Kingdom, BREEAM is used in more than 50 countries, with over 1 million development projects registered.

Leadership in Energy and Environmental Design (LEED). LEED is the green rating system developed by the U.S. Green Building Council, and it has certified 53,000 projects in 135 countries. LEED-ND applies sustainability and smart growth principles to the neighborhood scale. Criteria for design practices and building materials are intended to improve occupants' physical, mental, and emotional well-being and sense of community and provide a foundation for a healthy lifestyle.

Rating systems that focus on the health aspects of buildings and communities are still being developed and include the following systems:

Blue Zones. The Blue Zones Communities certification process is based on the research of Dan Buettner and a National Geographic team that identified areas of the world where people tend to live long lives (referred to as Blue Zones) and the characteristics of those communities that contribute to good health. The process requires different sectors of the community (citizens, schools, employers, restaurants, grocery stores, and community leaders) to work together to meet health-related goals. Blue Zones Communities certification applies to entire cities or towns through the individual certification of a certain percentage of work sites, restaurants, schools, and grocery stores, and of citizens who commit to the process. In 2013, 14 U.S. communities were Blue Zone certified.

STAR Communities. Sustainability Tools for Assessing and Rating Communities (STAR Communities) is a voluntary rating framework designed for local governments that focuses on improving the livability and sustainability of communities in North America. The STAR framework has seven categories (the built environment; climate and energy; economy and jobs; education, arts, and community; equity and empowerment; health and safety; and natural systems) that together present a vision for how communities can become healthier, more prosperous, and more inclusive. More than 30 municipalities in the United States and Canada participated in the pilot program between November 2012 and October 2013.

WELL Building Standard. The WELL Building Standard is a health-based building certification standard that considers the impact of the built environment on human health in order to create the conditions for optimized wellness. Since 2007, Manhattan real estate firm Delos has joined with the Columbia Medical School, Cleveland Clinic, and Mayo Clinic, as well as leading architects, scientists, and wellness thought leaders, to create the protocol. The standard is performance based, with specific measurable markers that indicate successful compliance in seven categories—air, water, nourishment, light, fitness, comfort, and mind. The standard is designed to operate in conjunction with sustainability standards such as LEED. Recently, Delos helped implement WELL certification at CBRE's global headquarters in downtown Los Angeles.

Location Choices

A key principle of good land use is location, and healthy buildings ideally are located close to public transit and within a mixed-use framework of streets, sidewalks, and bikeways, with connections to food markets, schools, workplaces, open space and parks, and other places people go daily.

The principles of healthy building are similar to traditional "intuitive building" principles. Consideration of the context of the building—including a thoughtful relationship to the street and neighboring buildings and an orientation that allows access to natural light and fresh air—is also important.

Greener, Healthier Buildings

Building greener, with design and materials that reduce indoor air pollution, use less energy, and use recycled or renewable materials, is inherently healthier for people.

Green building rating and assessment programs have criteria for healthy orientation, design, materials, and construction (see feature box for more on these programs).

Other building programs, such as Passive House and zero-net-energy buildings, go further by reducing or eliminating energy costs through insulation, tight construction, and new heating and cooling technologies.

Passive solar exposure and large operable windows promote healthy orientation to daylight, keep fresh air flowing, and can reduce energy costs.

Green roofs produce multiple climate, health, and economic benefits: They provide insulation that lowers energy demand and utility costs, and they reduce noise and the

PROJECTS THAT WORK FOR HEALTH

The Bullitt Center, Seattle, Washington

The Bullitt Center, a six-story 50,000-square-foot commercial office building designed by Seattle's Miller Hull Partnership, may be the greenest office building in the world.

Located at the edge of the Capitol Hill neighborhood, conducive to pedestrian, bike, and transit-friendly lifestyles, this $30 million Living Building Challenge model features composting toilets, strict energy and water budgets, and no on-site parking. The Bullitt Foundation and its partners, Miller Hull and developer Point32, hope to demonstrate that a carbon-neutral office building can be commercially viable and aesthetically pleasing without placing onerous demands on its occupants.

Opened for tenants in April 2013, the center is closely monitored, with a kiosk in the exhibition space showing real-time measurements like indoor air quality, energy consumption, photovoltaic power production, and water levels. Scanning quick-response codes with smartphones reveals how the building is performing.

The green roof collects rainwater, which is stored in a large underground cistern and is used throughout the building. A solar array will generate as much electricity as the building uses. Inviting stairways, operable windows, and building materials containing no red-list materials promote a healthy office environment. Handsome architecture, native plantings, large structural timbers, and a revitalized pocket park connect the building naturally and aesthetically to the street and neighborhood.

The Bullitt Center in Seattle, designed by Miller Hull, opened on Earth Day 2013. (©Nic Lehoux)

The Breathe Easy homes at the High Point development in Seattle have been shown to alleviate occupants' asthma symptoms. (Seattle Housing Authority)

Green roof terraces at Hysan Place, a sustainable commercial building in Hong Kong, provide oases for building occupants and openings for breezes to pass through. (Grischa Rüschendorf)

urban heat-island effect. Green roofs cleanse and reduce stormwater runoff, create open space for community gatherings and recreation, and provide natural areas and community gardens. Green roofs typically cost more to install, but they create value by extending the life of the roof membrane and reducing the long-term costs of heating and cooling buildings.

Seattle Housing Authority's High Point Healthy Homes and Community, a mixed-use affordable-housing community developed by Enterprise Community Partners, proved that design strategies can improve health. The community suffered from a high rate of asthma, so a team led by Mithun designed 60 "Breathe Easy" homes with features that improved indoor air quality and construction that decreased asthma risk factors. Studies showed that residents of Breathe Easy homes experienced 61 percent more symptom-free days and 67 percent fewer emergency room visits.

INSIGHTS FROM THE EXPERTS

Bert Gregory, Chairman and CEO, Mithun

Bert Gregory, FAIA, LEED AP BD+C, has led the architecture firm Mithun to national recognition for concept-based, environmentally intelligent design.

Q: *How do buildings work within neighborhoods in terms of sustainability factors?*

A: To maximize potential and minimize waste, a neighborhood or city should be viewed much like a natural ecosystem: interconnected and working as an economic, environmental, and social system. Great places feed on the synergy of many things.

Our study for the Lloyd Crossing EcoDistrict in Portland, Oregon, introduced the concept of "predevelopment metrics," a methodology for benchmarking and measuring habitat, water, and energy use, and an urban environment that mimics natural systems and reduces the development's net environmental impact over time. Our EcoDistrict approach also offers a sustainable financial model for investments in the whole system—buildings, urban infrastructure, and the natural environment—to achieve water, energy, carbon, and habitat goals.

Q: *Which of Mithun's built projects embodies what it means to be a healthy building?*

A: The Seattle Housing Authority's High Point Healthy Homes and Community initiative through the Breathe Easy Home Demonstration Project featured homes that decreased the risk factors that cause asthma among low-income children. We used positive pressure ventilation with air filtration, flooring that reduces allergens, low-VOC [volatile organic compound] and formaldehyde-free materials, and special landscaping and construction sequencing.

Q: *What's next in healthy building design?*

A: The movement toward healthy neighborhoods and the advancement of what "healthy" means in the built environment will emerge from evidence-based design and Health Impact Assessments. Facts and metrics will drive design and transparency in the chemical composition of materials and products, promotion of good ergonomics and physical activity, and a wider understanding of the importance of "nonbuilt" aspects of healthy living.

In the next few decades, we'll see the intersection of health, sustainability, and livability. Urban environments are at the center of these issues. Great real estate development, city and community advocacy, nonprofit leadership, and high-quality design can contribute to the creation of highly livable, compact, connected, and healthy buildings and neighborhoods—the creation of great places that make us feel better, and that enrich the soul.

Great real estate development, city and community advocacy, nonprofit leadership, and high-quality design can contribute to the creation of highly livable, compact, connected, and healthy buildings and neighborhoods—the creation of great places that make us feel better, and that enrich the soul.

—Bert Gregory

INNOVATIONS IN HEALTH

Active Design Guidelines for Buildings

New York City's Active Design Guidelines offer design strategies to promote active living within buildings.

Recommendations include the following:

- **Stairs.** Increase the use of stairs by providing a conveniently located staircase for everyday use, posting motivational signs, and designing visible, appealing, comfortable stairs.
- **Building functions.** Locate building functions to encourage brief bouts of walking to shared spaces, such as mail rooms and lunchrooms, and to provide appealing, supportive walking routes within buildings.
- **Exercise facilities.** Provide facilities that support exercise, such as centrally visible physical activity spaces, showers, locker rooms, secure bicycle storage, and drinking fountains.
- **Exteriors.** Design building exteriors and massing that contribute to a pedestrian-friendly urban environment, and include variety, transparency, multiple entries, outdoor seating, and canopies.

New York City provides these motivational posters free to any building that will display them. (NYC Department of Health and Mental Hygiene)

Designing for Active Living

Elements such as inviting facades, welcoming entrances from the street, and resident gathering places—attractive lobbies, communal kitchens, and comfortable libraries and media rooms—encourage social interaction in apartments, condominiums, and senior housing and health care facilities.

Spire, a new 40-story luxury green condominium building located within the theater and convention district in downtown Denver, became one of the fastest-selling towers in the United States in 2012. Among its active-living amenities are a health club, rooftop pool and spa, terrace with a grilling area, bike storage, on-site car share, and a perfect walk score of 100.

Interior features in public and commercial buildings, such as prominent and attractive staircases, encourage people to fit more exercise into their daily routine.

Universal design features support accessibility for all people, including those with disabilities as well as seniors. Design features include level entrances or ramps from the street, layouts with the master bedroom on the main level, and features such as wider doorways and hallways to accommodate wheelchairs and grab bars in showers. Universal design features in many cases can be retrofitted into buildings.

Attractive interior staircases can encourage people to take the stairs rather than the elevator. (©Nic Lehoux)

Reworking Workplaces

Companies are investing in healthy workplaces to attract talented employees, reduce absenteeism, and provide an environment that is lively and collaborative and that provides some key daily necessities, including healthy food and opportunities for breaks, recreation, and socializing, all in one location.

Recent research on the harmful effects of sitting for hours every day and the importance of movement, especially frequent periods of aerobic activity, to maintain physical and cognitive health has prompted companies to rethink their office spaces and routines.

Silicon Valley's high-tech industry is among the leaders in creating healthy office environments. Workplaces such as Google's headquarters feature active and contemplative spaces—volleyball and bocce courts, yoga and meditation rooms, and multiuse path networks to connect buildings and encourage employees to stay active, fit, destressed, and creative.

Healthy Learning Environments

Children are more vulnerable than adults to both outdoor and indoor air pollutants. Because children spend so much time in school buildings, the school environment can have a big impact on their health.

School siting is critical, as schools located near busy roads have been found to have high levels of indoor pollutants. Designs for new school buildings are featuring operable windows and skylights. Students who studied in classrooms with more natural light scored up to 25 percent higher on standardized tests. Buildings with improved air quality reduced asthma incidence in students by nearly 40 percent.

Green School Buildings Have Many Benefits

Financial benefits of green schools (dollars per square foot)

Increased earnings	$49
Energy	$9
Cold and flu reduction	$5
Teacher retention	$4
Asthma reduction	$3
Employment impact	$2
Emissions	$1
Water and wastewater	$1
Total	**$74**
Cost of improvements	**$3**
Net financial benefits	**$71**

Source: U.S. Green Building Council.

PROJECTS THAT WORK FOR HEALTH

Googleplex, Mountain View, California

The mantra of healthy buildings has guided Google's interior redesign and renovations of scores of buildings at the Googleplex corporate headquarters in Silicon Valley. The high-tech giant approaches healthy workplaces as an imperative for attracting and retaining the best and brightest workers, and for encouraging innovation, collaboration, and productivity. Google's design approach for its Silicon Valley building works to counter some of the disadvantages of its suburban location.

Google's interiors feature flexible space that encourages movement, creativity, and communal socializing and meals, with large open spaces for meetings and a variety of much smaller "cuddle" spaces for private discussion and phone conversations. Google's own Green Team researches construction materials and furnishings, maintaining a custom red list of toxic materials.

Google employees are encouraged to stay active with interior slides, beach volleyball, a bowling alley, a climbing wall, seven fitness centers, and a fleet of campus bikes and scooters, including seven-person "conference bikes." On-site lockers and showers facilitate cleanup. Over 25 cafeterias and cafés offer locally sourced gourmet lunches.

Google Apps help track progress toward green goals, which meet or exceed LEED standards with technology such as solar panels and solar hot water heaters, as well as dual-stage air filtration systems to improve air quality.

The redesigned Google headquarters in Mountain View, California, incorporates a number of features that encourage employees to stay healthy and active, including fleets of "G-bikes." (Bloomberg/ Getty Images)

BY THE NUMBERS

Working for Health

23% Percentage of U.S. office workers who experience symptoms of sick building syndrome

15% Potential increase in U.S. worker productivity through greater access to sunlight in office buildings

54% Percentage of U.S. workplaces reported to have an on-site gym or fitness area

3.1 million Decrease in the number of calories consumed by Google's New York City office over seven weeks when free candy was placed in opaque containers and healthy snacks in glass jars

Sources: *ASHRAE Journal*; National Renewable Energy Laboratory; International Facility Management Association; Google Inc.

PROJECTS THAT WORK FOR HEALTH

Alder Hey Children's Health Park, Liverpool, England

Alder Hey in the Park, due to open in 2015, is a 270-bed children's hospital designed with the help of patients and their families and built by the Acorn Consortium (John Laing, Laing O'Rourke, and Interserve).

The facility has 48 critical care beds for patients needing special care, access to play areas, natural light, and views of the site's large park. Most rooms will be private, and every ward will have a kitchen that prepares fresh food to order.

Once fully constructed, the Alder Hey Children's Health Park in Liverpool, England, will intertwine nature and park space with hospital buildings. (BDP)

Health Care Facilities

Health care facilities are evolving. Hospitals are extending their campuses and adding rehabilitation centers and nursing homes. Larger medical centers with strong medical schools and research capacities are joining up with practicing hospitals.

Hospitals and other large health care facilities serve as anchor institutions for communities, not only by providing health services but also by serving as employment centers and forces for economic development, community health, and neighborhood revitalization.

HealthPlan Services, a services company to the managed-care and health insurance industries, announced plans to bring 1,000 new jobs to Tampa, Florida, with a related $34 million capital investment in a new 96,000-square-foot facility.

In Spartanburg, South Carolina, the new campus of the Virginia-based Edward Via College of Osteopathic Medicine has helped spur community partnerships and a redevelopment opportunity for the city's Northside neighborhood, a high-poverty and high-crime area of the city lacking many health-promoting built-environment features.

The health care sector can also contribute through adaptive reuse of existing, centrally located buildings. The Kingwood Medical Center in Houston, Texas, originally built as a shopping mall, was converted to a hospital and office building.

Health facilities are also moving into retail spaces and lobby areas of office towers. Bringing health care closer to patients is part of the new health care law, and it offers new opportunities within the real estate sector. Real estate services company Jones Lang LaSalle recently reported that health care office space is one of the most sought after real estate sectors.

CHAPTER 6

Access to Healthy Food

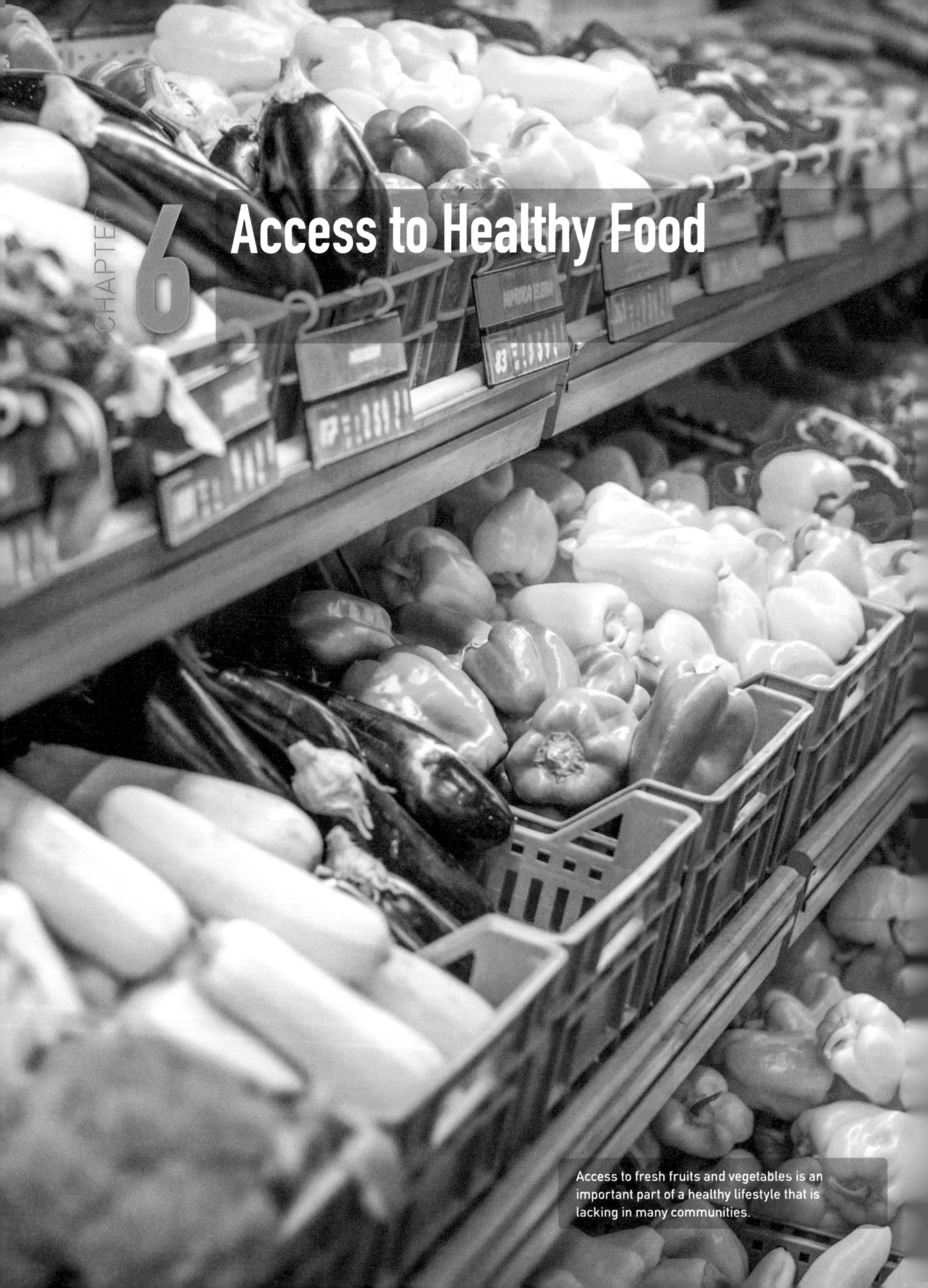

Access to fresh fruits and vegetables is an important part of a healthy lifestyle that is lacking in many communities.

Good nutrition establishes a healthy foundation for life, particularly in the first three years, which are critical to children's physical and mental health, academic achievement, and economic productivity.

Healthy communities flourish with access to healthy food through a variety of places, including grocery stores, urban farms, community gardens, and farmers markets. Housing and workplaces located near full-service supermarkets, for example, are linked to lower obesity rates.

About 870 million people, or 12.5 percent of the global population, were undernourished in 2012, with the vast majority living in developing countries. Even in the United States, 50 million people—including one in every five children—went hungry in 2011.

INNOVATIONS IN HEALTH

Urban Farming, Detroit, Michigan

Urban Farming is a global nonprofit organization that started with three gardens in Detroit and now has over 62,000 gardens in more than 20 countries. The organization provides free gardening and educational resources to families and individuals around the world.

The Urban Farming gardens and farms are located in urban, suburban, and rural areas. The organization encourages people to grow their own food so that they may move beyond challenges of unemployment, malnourishment, food insecurity, or hunger. Plant giveaways help families and individuals start their own gardens so they can reduce their monthly grocery bills and begin to incorporate healthy eating into their lifestyle.

Urban Farming's plant giveaways help residents of low-income urban neighborhoods start growing produce at home.
(Courtesy of Urban Farming)

Food Insecurity Varies by Race and Is Very High in Households below the Poverty Threshold

Percentage of households facing food insecurity, by selected household characteristics

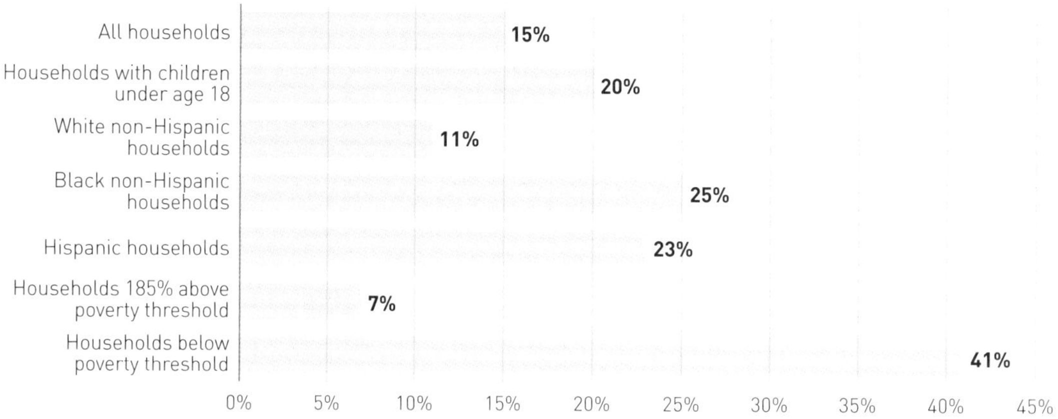

Source: U.S. Department of Agriculture.

Note: The USDA defines food insecurity as limited or uncertain access to adequate food.

BY THE NUMBERS

Healthy Food

1,500 Number of calories in a typical fast-food meal

175% Increase in the number of U.S. farmers markets from 2000 to 2012

15% Percentage of the world's food grown in urban areas (including backyard and rooftop gardens and community gardens)

10 Average number of pounds a person loses in a year by lowering daily calorie intake by 100

Sources: U.S. Department of Agriculture; Obesity Action Coalition; Harvard School of Public Health.

At the same time, obesity has reached epidemic levels, affecting 500 million adults worldwide in 2008.

Obesity can be caused by a lack of access to healthy food because of its cost—healthier foods like fresh organic fruits and vegetables often cost more than junk food—and because of food production, processing, distribution, and marketing practices.

The lack of access is profound in "food deserts"—typically lower-income urban, suburban, or rural areas without a full-service grocery store or other sources of fresh healthy food.

Convenience stores, corner markets, bodegas, street vendors, and fast-food restaurants are often the only available and affordable food sources in urban neighborhoods. But many of their food items, such as soda and chips, are higher in fat, sugar, salt, and chemical additives, compared with healthier choices.

INNOVATIONS IN HEALTH

Fresh Food Retailer Initiative, New Orleans, Louisiana

In March 2011, the city of New Orleans began the Fresh Food Retailer Initiative, a financing program aimed at increasing the number of supermarkets, grocery stores, and other fresh-food markets in low-income and underserved communities. The city started the program to address a lack of fresh healthy foods in many New Orleans neighborhoods, a problem worsened by Hurricane Katrina.

The Fresh Food Retailer Initiative enables operators to open, renovate, or expand retail outlets that sell fresh fruits and vegetables. Working with local partners, the program offers financing for food markets in communities where infrastructure costs and credit needs cannot be filled by conventional financial institutions.

Convenience stores in urban neighborhoods often lack fresh, healthy, and affordable food options.

Crossing the Food Desert: Grocery Stores

Introducing a full-service grocery store into an urban neighborhood provides a source of healthier food. It also creates jobs and an anchor for other commercial development, which further increases retail activity, job growth, and property values in the surrounding neighborhoods.

Public/private partnerships are working in some cities to develop full-service grocery stores and to add fresh foods to corner stores and bodegas in communities without access to healthful foods.

Incentives to draw grocery stores to urban neighborhoods are especially effective in locations on pedestrian-friendly main-street corridors, close to transit-oriented development, and on mixed-use sites with affordable

PROJECTS THAT WORK FOR HEALTH

Union Market, Washington, D.C.

Developed by Edens, Union Market has become a hotspot for a hip new food scene in Northeast Washington. Located in a 24-acre wholesale food district in an emerging part of the city, the 25,000-square-foot market houses 40 local vendors, including a bakery, a creamery, several butchers, a wine shop, and a knife-sharpening business.

The new Union Market occupies the same site as a historic market. Because of damage to the existing building, Edens built an almost entirely new structure with a modern, inviting interior. Union Market has added life to the existing warehouse district by hosting local food entrepreneurs trying out new food concepts. Edens is now working with local landowners and the city to re-develop other segments of the wholesale market district with residential and commercial uses.

Union Market in Northeast Washington, D.C., provides space for food entrepreneurs. (Douglas Graham/Getty Images)

INNOVATIONS IN HEALTH

Healthy Food Chain, Boulder, Colorado

Boulder, recognized as one of the healthiest cities in the United States, has developed a vibrant culture around local food production and distribution, as well as nationally recognized farm-to-table restaurants. Links in Boulder's healthy food chain include the following:

- **Boulder Farmers Market** offers fresh organic produce, dairy products, baked goods, and locally raised meat. Vendors accept government-subsidized food program vouchers to make food more affordable for low-income households.
- **Growing Gardens,** a nonprofit organization located on farmland leased to the city, manages community garden plots at 11 sites, a produce-growing program for a countywide food pantry, summer camps, a CSA, and a farm-job program for local teens who sell the produce at the farmers market.
- **Boulder Food Rescue** arranges for volunteers to pick up just-expired organic produce, baked goods, and cooked meals from grocery stores and cafés and deliver them daily by bikes with trailers to 25 agencies that feed hungry, homeless, and low-income populations.
- The city's **zoning code** was amended in 2012 to allow urban agriculture uses in all zones throughout the city, including in parks and city rights-of-way.

housing. Homes located in proximity to new grocery stores have been found to increase in value by 5 to 7 percent.

Progress Plaza in North Philadelphia was vacant for ten years as the owners struggled to find a grocery store operator for the low-medium-income urban market. In 2009, TRF, a community development financial institution, provided New Markets Tax Credit financing to support the construction and permanent financing for a supermarket and retail center. The new 46,000-square-foot Fresh Grocer full-service supermarket brought affordable healthy food choices to the community, as well as 272 jobs.

At the 63rd Street Farm in Boulder, Colorado, members pick up weekly food shares produced at the farm. (Cyrus McCrimmon/Getty Images)

PROJECTS THAT WORK FOR HEALTH

Willowsford, Loudoun County, Virginia

The master-planned community of Willowsford, located in rural Loudon County, has 4,000 rolling acres of fields and woods that are drawing homeowners who are attracted to the 400-acre organic farm, more than 2,000 acres of conservation land, and healthy and active-living amenities.

In 2009, developer Corbelis of Boston purchased the four parcels, which had an approved master plan focusing on a golf course with 2,200 dispersed single-family homes. Corbelis looked at the farmland and envisioned an organic farm woven through four compact residential villages and surrounded by preserved land.

Beginning in 2011, construction was front-loaded for the farm, two pools and clubhouses, a spray-and-play park, fitness facilities, and a village green framed by decorative gardens. The active-living concept is selling briskly, at a premium of $20 per square foot over other residential communities in the area. The project was selected as the National Association of Home Builders' top community in 2012.

The nonprofit Willowsford Conservancy manages the parks and open space, planned with 45 miles of trails and interpretive natural areas. The clubhouses feature demonstration kitchens with a culinary director and farm-to-table cooking classes. Residents volunteer at the farm, purchase fresh produce at the farm stand, share in the CSA operation, and gather for farm workshops and potluck dinners.

The CSA's first season in 2012 produced 200 varieties of vegetables and fruits; poultry and livestock are planned as part of the operation. Managed by an experienced organic farmer, the farm is expected to begin paying for itself within four years.

Residents of Willowsford in Loudoun County, Virginia, have access to the Willowsford Farm, which supports the community with healthy food and acts as a hub for community engagement. (Deborah Dramby/Willowsford Farm)

Investments in urban food markets can become a generator for economic development. For example, the new Union Market in Northeast Washington, D.C., developed by Edens, is not only successful in its own right, but it is also advancing the regeneration of the area.

The Eco-Farmers Market at CityCentre in Houston provides local and in-season food. (ULI Houston)

The Number of U.S. Farmers Markets Has Nearly Tripled Since 2000

Number of U.S. farmers markets

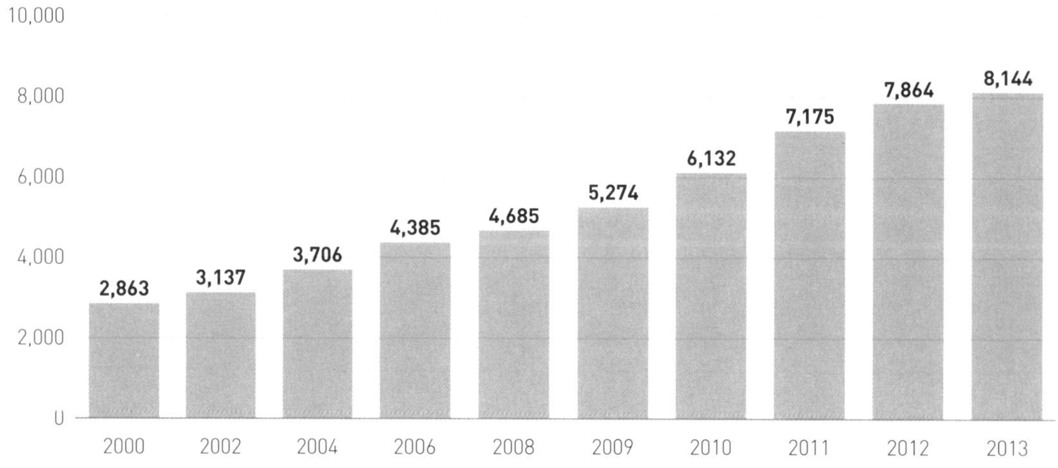

Source: U.S. Department of Agriculture.

Urban Agriculture

Urban agriculture is especially important in low-income communities, where it has the greatest impact on reducing poverty and hunger. From Detroit to Cape Town, urban farms and community gardens are producing food for families and cash crops that are integrated into local markets to help meet food demand, provide income, and open up opportunities for buying locally produced goods.

An estimated 18,000 community gardens in the United States, most of which are owned and managed by local governments and nonprofit organizations, provide plots where people can grow produce.

Farmers markets are another part of the worldwide movement to encourage production and distribution of local food, a movement that also includes community-supported agriculture (CSA). In the United States, the number of registered farmers markets has grown at a fast pace, more than doubling since 2006, to 8,144 in 2013, reports the U.S. Department of Agriculture.

INNOVATIONS IN HEALTH

Urban Gardens, Cape Town, South Africa

In poor townships in Cape Town, local food is being looked to for solutions. Abalimi Bezekhaya is a voluntary association that works for sustainable food production and environmental greening in poor townships on the Cape Flats, a sprawling area of 1 million residents in metropolitan Cape Town. The organization has helped residents establish 2,500 home vegetable gardens and nearly 100 community group projects, such as planting school gardens and street trees.

Abalimi—which means "the planters" in the Xhosa language—provides training and gardening supplies, such as tools, seeds, manure, organic pest control, and plants. The group supports individual households, especially women who represent whole families, in establishing organic gardens and microfarming and conservation projects.

At Abalimi's packing center, workers wash, sort, and pack vegetables into preordered boxes to be delivered to well-off Cape Town suburbs. In an area with 40 percent unemployment, the gardens have improved household diets, boosted the local economy, and added sustainable income streams for 3,000 microfarmers.

Abalimi Bezekhaya microfarmers prepare Harvest of Hope "seed-to-table" vegetable boxes in Cape Town, South Africa. (Cynthia E. Smith, Smithsonian Institution, photo from Cooper-Hewitt, National Design Museum's "Design with the Other 90%: CITIES" exhibition)

CHAPTER 7

Clear Air, Clean Water

Village women transport clean water in Khajuraho, India.

Air and water quality are directly affected by the built environment and have direct impacts on human health. Across the globe, cities and countries are facing extreme health challenges from outdoor air pollution and a lack of clean and safe drinking water and appropriate sanitation infrastructure.

Investments in public transit systems to help reduce the number of cars on the road and building practices that help reduce runoff that pollutes lakes and rivers are ways that the development industry can help alleviate these serious issues.

BY THE NUMBERS

The Importance of Clean Air and Water

780 million
Number of people globally who lack access to clean drinking water

3.4 million
Number of people globally who die each year from a water-related disease

15%
Increase in mortality rate in cities with high levels of air pollution compared with cleaner cities

Sources: Water.org; World Health Organization.

Air Quality

Air pollution is one of the most deadly by-products of modern industrialization, nonrenewable energy consumption, and car-centric development. Practices such as burning coal for heat and electricity, producing cement and steel, and refining oil can damage air quality with toxic substances, as well as suspended particles—dust, soot, or chemicals—that lodge in the lungs.

To combat air pollution in Beijing, the city is investing in transit, regulating emissions from fuel, limiting car purchases, and restricting driving.

Urban areas are prone to higher levels of asthma and other respiratory diseases linked to air pollution from industry, vehicle exhaust, and a lack of air circulation in dense vertical environments. More than half the U.S. population lives in areas that do not meet air quality standards set by the EPA.

Air pollution can also cause emphysema, strokes, heart attacks, and cancers. Lead exposure in young children from sources such as fuel exhaust has been linked to complications later in life, including lower IQ, hyperactivity, behavioral problems, learning disabilities, and juvenile delinquency.

Air pollution is a particularly difficult challenge in China. Poor air quality contributed to 1.2 million premature deaths in China in 2010, nearly 40 percent of the global total. Along with other Chinese cities, the capital Beijing struggles with air pollution issues stemming from a dramatic rise in industry and cars, as well as air inversions that trap pollutants and particulates.

Clearing the air of pollution and maintaining healthy air quality pose challenges in many cities and regions globally, especially in the developing world. Reducing toxic and particulate-laden vehicle and industrial emissions and developing green solutions to clear the air are among the most important ways of achieving healthy communities.

Although some air pollution solutions require government regulation and funding, developers can help improve outdoor air quality by locating projects in urban transit-served neighborhoods to reduce driving and associated emissions, and by supporting efforts to build multimodal transportation systems.

Without Serious Reforms, Air Pollution Levels in China Could Worsen Dramatically

Particulate matter levels forecast for China versus WHO standard and levels in selected countries

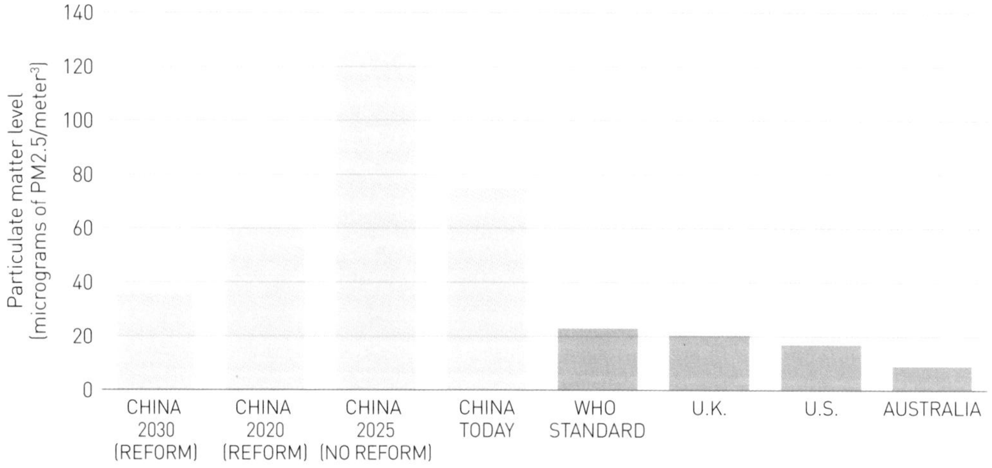

Source: Deutsche Bank.

INSIGHTS FROM THE EXPERTS

Simon Ng, Head of Transport and Sustainability Research, Civic Exchange, Hong Kong

Simon Ng is Head of Transport and Sustainability Research for Civic Exchange, a public policy organization working to reduce air pollution in Hong Kong, one of the world's densest cities. Hong Kong suffers from severe air pollution, despite a world-class public transportation system on which 90 percent of daily passenger trips are made.

Q: *What are the impacts of poor air quality on the human, economic, and social health of Hong Kong?*

A: Poor air quality is a major health risk, and more so for the elderly, children, pregnant women, and people with health complaints like asthma. Studies show that low-income residents are extremely vulnerable. Improving air quality is a win-win opportunity. Society will benefit, as clean air will reduce health care costs, increase productivity, improve long-term competitiveness, attract tourists and overseas talents, and create new jobs.

Q: *What changes in the built environment and transportation are needed to improve the air quality?*

A: We need to clean up the vehicles by using cleaner fuel/energy, replacing old and polluting vehicles, and retrofitting in-use ones with emission-reduction devices. To think long term for lasting impacts, we need to encourage public transport over private cars, promote walking and cycling, and enhance integrated transport and land use planning to reduce the number of vehicle journeys.

Q: *How can Hong Kong's clean air efforts provide a model for developing countries?*

A: Hong Kong has both successful and less successful stories about reducing emissions from power plants and road vehicles. For example, Hong Kong will be the first in Asia to regulate ship emissions. In that process, Civic Exchange has been instrumental in translating scientific research into industry's voluntary action, and then in helping secure government regulation. Technology, regulation, and public/private collaboration are all important.

To think long term for lasting impacts, we need to encourage public transport over private cars, promote walking and cycling, and enhance integrated transport and land use planning to reduce the number of vehicle journeys.

—Simon Ng

INNOVATIONS IN HEALTH

Clearing the Air in Mexico City, Mexico

In 1992, when high ozone levels led to 1,000 deaths and 35,000 hospitalizations, Mexico City was declared the most polluted city on the planet. Since then, sprawling urban development and car ownership have increased; some 6.2 million trips are made by car every day.

In this same time span, however, Mexico City's harmful ozone levels have dropped 75 percent, with carbon monoxide and other air pollutants declining. The presence of lead has been reduced by 90 percent since 1990.

How has Mexico City successfully cleared its air? It has done so by reducing pollutants, expanding transit, and greening the city. The state oil company started selling lower-sulfur and unleaded gasoline, while the No Driving Today program keeps cars off the road one day a week. A large oil refinery was closed and converted into a park.

The city is building Metro Line 12, with 20 new stations and three Metrobus transfer centers. The new metro line will transport about 450,000 passengers daily and features transit-oriented development, including public health facilities and bike parks. The city launched a bike-share system that now has 70 stations and 73,000 members.

The government offers a tax incentive of 10 percent of the value of the building for installing green roofs; over 225,000 square feet of green roofs have been installed on public buildings and private establishments.

Water for Life

Water quality and sanitation in the built environment—including clean water infrastructure, sanitary disposal of human waste, effective stormwater management, and water pollution mitigation—have a significant impact on health, sustainable growth, and development of communities.

Establishing and maintaining clean drinking water and adequate sanitation systems require careful attention to water supply, rainwater drainage, solid-waste disposal, and human-waste disposal.

Worldwide, nearly 1 billion people lack access to an adequate water supply. By 2025, water scarcity will affect nearly two-thirds of the world's population, threatening basic health aspects like food production.

Mexico City has made strong progress in addressing its air pollution problem.

Young women collect water from a well in a village in Senegal.

More than 2.5 billion people globally lack access to basic sanitary waste services. Unsafe water supplies and inadequate sanitation and hygiene can lead to deadly diseases, including diarrhea, dysentery, cholera, hepatitis, and typhoid. Some 1.8 million people die every year from diarrheal diseases; 90 percent of them are children under age five, mostly in developing countries.

With the rise of "megacities," urban population growth, especially in slums, often exceeds governments' ability to meet water needs through new infrastructure and improvements.

Across the globe, highways and buildings constructed along waterfronts, rivers, wetlands, and coastlines can be sources of water pollution. Buildings, streets, sidewalks,

INNOVATIONS IN HEALTH

Community Sanitation Blocks, Mumbai, India

Megacity Mumbai cannot keep up with infrastructure demands of a population that has grown to 20 million. Despite its growing wealth, Mumbai has 6 million people living in slums. A community-led sanitation block program is addressing their need for clean water and toilets.

In the mid-1980s, Mahila Milan ("women together"), collectives of women slum and pavement dwellers, joined with the National Slum Dwellers Federation and the Society for the Promotion of Area Resource Centres to build community toilet blocks in Mumbai's slums.

In 2000, the Municipal Corporation of Greater Mumbai, with a World Bank loan and grants from the Bill and Melinda Gates Foundation, expanded the project. So far, over 360 toilet blocks have been constructed, serving over 360,000 residents. The program's target is to provide toilet facilities for 1 million slum dwellers.

The World Bank's National Water and Sanitation Program has brought better water and sanitation services to places like rural Azerbaijan. (World Bank Photo Collection)

parking lots, and other impervious surfaces cause stormwater runoff to carry harmful pathogens and chemicals into rivers, lakes, and other water sources.

In New York Harbor, for example, more than 27 billion gallons of raw sewage and polluted stormwater are discharged annually from combined sewer overflows (CSOs), according to the Riverkeepers, a clean water advocacy organization. Rain can overload outmoded sewer systems, which combine sewage from buildings with dirty stormwater from streets. CSOs are a major water pollution concern for cities that have combined sewer systems. Preventing and managing CSOs can be costly for local governments.

As climate change affects the built environment with more volatile stormwater surges and flooding, maintaining clean water sources and separated sanitary waste systems will become even more critical. About 3.7 million people living along the East and West Coasts of the United States, for example, will be affected by more frequent coastal flooding from sea level rise in coming decades.

INNOVATIONS IN HEALTH

Watershed Management Group and Tucson's Green Streets Policy

Capturing stormwater is an important source for landscape irrigation in the arid Southwest. In 2008, the Watershed Management Group, a nonprofit organization that works in Tucson and Phoenix, Arizona, and other Sonoran Desert communities, launched its Green Streets/Green Neighborhoods program to demonstrate how to use stormwater to provide a cooler and more active city and to reduce flooding.

The organization's efforts resulted in the 2013 City of Tucson Green Streets Policy, which requires all new and redeveloped roads to be designed to capture stormwater to grow street trees.

The policy is intended to increase Tucson's tree canopy coverage from 5 percent to 25 percent along new roadways and to reduce the city's urban heat-island effect. The green streets are also intended to filter air and water pollution, to provide appealing sidewalks and lanes for walking and biking, to create connections with the natural world, to beautify the city, and to increase real estate values.

Tucson, Arizona's Green Streets Policy requires integrated stormwater-harvesting systems, such as vegetated streetside basins. (Watershed Management Group)

Green Infrastructure

Green infrastructure, also known as low-impact development or stormwater harvesting, benefits public health by improving air and water quality and can save cities and developers money.

Trees and plants improve air quality by removing toxins, such as carbon monoxide and ozone, linked to respiratory problems. Urban parks help cool cities and combat the urban heat-island effect, in which impervious surfaces, including streets, buildings, and parking lots, absorb heat and radiate it back into the environment.

A rain garden and cistern are examples of the green infrastructure at the ECO Modern Flats in Fayetteville, Arkansas. (Timothy Hursley)

Green Roofs Have a Wide Range of Community Benefits

Benefits of green roofs

Source: Adapted from WellHome.

Natural stormwater management areas, such as bioretention ponds and bioswales, which use plants and soil to absorb runoff and filter pollutants, are being constructed in parks, parking lots, tree lawns, and other urban areas. Green stormwater management and air pollution reduction in parks help save Philadelphia $16 million annually, according to the Trust for Public Land.

Permeable paving, which allows stormwater to infiltrate paved surfaces to recharge groundwater, can eliminate the need for costly conventional drainage systems.

Green roofs can absorb up to 90 percent of stormwater and save on long-term operating costs. (See chapter 5.)

Underground cisterns connected to building downspouts can capture and store rainwater to be pumped out for irrigation. Graywater, or wastewater from sinks, showers, and baths, can be recycled on site to flush toilets or irrigate landscapes.

PROJECTS THAT WORK FOR HEALTH

Silver City Townhomes, Milwaukee, Wisconsin

Silver City Townhomes is a 42,000-square-foot urban infill development, constructed on the site of vacant city-owned parking lots and sports courts in an inner-city Milwaukee neighborhood. The 20 rent-to-own townhomes were designed and developed by Quorum Architects and Layton Boulevard West Neighbors Inc. to provide high-quality, energy-efficient, and affordable-housing options for working families that also helped revitalize the neighborhood. In 2011, Silver City Townhomes won a Milwaukee Award for Neighborhood Development Innovation, which recognizes projects that strengthen inner-city neighborhoods.

The project's signature green building element is a green roof installed on all five buildings and planted with multiple varieties of sedum. The city of Milwaukee struggles with an old combined sewer overflow system, and Silver City's green roofs have proved effective at reducing the volume of stormwater runoff, retaining an estimated 6,500 gallons per rain event.

The green roofs have also been successful at improving the thermal performance of the townhomes, reducing residents' utility bills by 20 percent. Visible at eye level from the adjacent 35th Street Viaduct, the roofs help market the project and Silver City's commitment to sustainability.

The Silver City Townhomes affordable-housing project in Milwaukee, Wisconsin, installed green roofs on all five residential buildings. (Silver City Townhomes LLC)

PROJECTS THAT WORK FOR HEALTH

Public Utilities Commission Headquarters, San Francisco, California

Opened in 2012, the LEED Platinum headquarters for San Francisco's Public Utilities Commission incorporates innovations in sustainability, reflecting its mission of providing and managing water, wastewater, and power for the San Francisco area. The 13-story, 277,000-square-foot office building, designed by KMD Architects and Stevens Architects, consumes 32 percent less energy than similarly sized buildings. A solar array and wind turbine generate power meeting up to 7 percent of the building's needs, and daylight harvesting saves electricity and minimizes artificial lighting.

One of the first U.S. buildings with on-site treatment of blackwater and graywater, the headquarters consumes 60 percent less water than similar buildings. A rainwater-harvesting system provides water for irrigation around the building, and 100 percent of wastewater is treated and recycled for the building's toilets.

The Public Utilities Commission headquarters in San Francisco incorporated a number of green building features, including on-site blackwater and graywater treatment. (KMD Architects and Bruce Damonte)

Adding It All Up: Elements of Healthy Development

Building design

Green roofs

Centrally placed, inviting, and accessible stairways

Operable windows

Healthy interior and exterior building materials

Views of nature and exposure to sunlight

Accessible design features

Building amenities

Workout spaces

Storage for bikes and other equipment

Lockers, bike racks, and places to shower

What would you add or change? What projects are you working on that include these elements? Share your thoughts on Twitter using #ulihealth.

Location and community

Compact land use and a mix of uses

Proximity to nature and high-quality parks and playgrounds

Programs that encourage activity and social interaction

Ready access to healthy food

Transportation

High-quality and reliable transit service

Walkable streets that accommodate all users

Bike trails and lanes

Gridded street patterns

Acknowledgments

The Building Healthy Places Initiative gratefully acknowledges the contributions of the following people to this report:

Erin Christensen Ishizaki, AIA, LEED AP ND
Associate Principal, Director
Mithun
Seattle, Washington

Laura Cole
Vice President of Marketing
Corbelis
Willowsford, Virginia

Anthony Davies
Associate Director
Buro Happold Ltd.
Bath, United Kingdom

Natasha Franck
Project Manager
Delos Living
New York, New York

Bert Gregory, FAIA, LEED AP BD+C
Chairman and CEO
Mithun
Seattle, Washington

Richard Jackson, MD, MPH, FAAP
Chair
Department of Environmental Health Sciences
University of California, Los Angeles
Los Angeles, California

Mark Johnson, FASLA
Founder and Principal
Civitas
Denver, Colorado

Ken Kay, FASLA
Founder and Principal
KenKay Associates
San Francisco, California

Bill LaPatra, AIA, LEED AP
Partner
Mithun
Seattle, Washington

Michael Leccese
Executive Director
ULI Colorado
Denver, Colorado

Jaclyn Lensen
Communications Manager, Healthy Living
Colorado Health Foundation
Denver, Colorado

Simon Ng
Head of Transport and Sustainability Research
Civic Exchange
Hong Kong

Jonathan F.P. Rose
President
Jonathan Rose Companies LLC
New York, New York

Tim Van Meter, AIA
Partner, Architect and Urban Designer
Van Meter Williams Pollack
Denver, Colorado

The Urban Land Institute is grateful to the Colorado Health Foundation for its support of the Building Healthy Places Initiative.